SKIN FOR SKIN
and
THE VERDICT
OF BRIDLEGOOSE

SKIN FOR SKIN

and

THE VERDICT
OF BRIDLEGOOSE

Llewelyn Powys

THE BODLEY HEAD · LONDON

Skin for Skin

First published 1926
This edition 1948

The Verdict of Bridlegoose

First published 1927
This edition 1948

Printed in Great Britain by
UNWIN BROTHERS LIMITED, LONDON AND WOKING
for JOHN LANE, THE BODLEY HEAD LIMITED
8 Bury Place, London, W.C.1

Contents

SKIN FOR SKIN

Contents

SKIN FOR SKIN

Dedicated

in admiration and devotion

to

Gertrude Mary Powys

AGAIN THERE was a day when the sons of God came to present themselves before the Lord, and Satan came also among them to present himself before the Lord.

And the Lord said unto Satan, From whence comest thou? And Satan answered the Lord, and said, From going to and fro in the Earth, and walking up and down in it.

And the Lord said unto Satan, Hast thou considered my servant Job, that *there is* none like him in the Earth, a perfect and an upright man, one that feareth God, and escheweth evil? and still he holdeth fast his integrity, although thou movedst me against him, to destroy him without cause.

And Satan answered the Lord and said, Skin for skin, yea, all that a man hath will he give for his life.

But put forth thine hand now, and touch his bone and his flesh and he will curse thee to thy face.

And the Lord said unto Satan, Behold he *is* in thine hand; but save his life.

CHAPTER ONE

A Churchyard Cough

I FIRST DISCOVERED that I had consumption during the small hours of a November night in the year 1909. All through that autumn I had been troubled by a bad cold, by a cold of that particularly virulent kind, persisting week after week, which is common enough in an English countryside where for months on end people inhale mists, move about in chilled rooms, and sleep between damp sheets. I had been lying awake for hours and never for a single moment had the rain ceased from lashing against the window-panes of my bedroom, never for a moment had the wind ceased from beating against the walls of the house, that wind which I knew, but a few minutes before, had been passing over Lenty Common, over Silver Lake, and over the lonely stretches of the Bradford Abbas road.

Suddenly, after a fit of coughing more violent than usual, an ugly conviction came over me that something was wrong. I lit a candle and discovered that my mouth was full of blood. The next day my worst misgivings were confirmed by a doctor. I was found to be suffering from pulmonary tuberculosis.

I was sent to bed; the two windows of my room being removed from their frames so that I should be able to have as much fresh air as possible until such a time as I could travel to Davos Platz, the famous Swiss health-resort.

I was twenty-five years old and little enough reconciled, God wot, to the possibility of dying. It seemed to me, during those first hours of my sickness, as though I had done nothing with my life, as though I had been guilty of allowing a priceless opportunity to pass by with the obtuseness of a veritable dizzard. Now, the scales having fallen from my eyes, I made the resolution that never again, never till I 'lay in hell like a sheep', would I suffer myself to be submerged by the commonplace. If only I was permitted to live one more year, two more years, how eagerly would I not mark the passage of the sun each day across the sky, the recurring phases of the treacherous moon, and the naked beauty of each starlit night!

For a month I lay in that small upper room, looking out through two gaping apertures at the bare branches of the elm trees in the school playing-fields. How well I knew the shape of each one of them! As a small boy I had sat under their shade on many a hot summer afternoon, watching cricket matches and munching chocolate. I could remember wedging silver paper into the crevices of their bark, bark which covered a timber used in Dorset, time out of mind, for the making of coffins.

And beyond the elms were 'The Slopes', leafless now, and appearing during those days sombre enough under the dense, sunless sky which hung like an enfolding pall over the Honeycombe Woods.

The shock of discovering myself to be really ill had the strangest effect on me. I became like one drunken with wine. A torrent of words issued from my mouth. I acted as if death were not the end of every child born into the world, but an event which in some mysterious way had been reserved for me alone. I felt nothing but pride in finding myself laid by the heels so neatly. I liked to get what sensation I could out of it; and yet, at the same time, deep in my heart, I refused to realise how grave my sickness was. I liked to talk about dying, but I had no mind to die. I liked to rail against God, but I had no mind that He should hear me. In every possible way I dramatised my situation. My head became completely turned, and I chittered at Death like a little grey squirrel who is up a fir tree out of harm's way.

My father came to see me and prayed at my bedside, his head white as the silver belly of a minnow, white as a dove's wing against a thunder-cloud. I watched him on his knees with the superficial arrogance of a bull calf who frisks away after looking over a meadow hedge at a yoked bullock, a bullock who, by an enforced abnegation of its own personal freedom, no longer makes claims upon life. I looked, I say, at the snow-white head of my father, at that head which possessed the dignity of a lion's head together with a lion's low forehead, and continued to indulge my mind in its own conceits, now and again glancing self-consciously at my pale hands lying motionless on the counterpane. Presently, when my father had finished his supplication and was no longer kneeling on the bare rain-washed boards which, from his Victorian point of view, were so unspeakably depressing, I persuaded him to read me certain poems of Matthew Arnold. 'He was not so good a man as his father,' he said emphatically, as he, at length, put down the thrice-precious volume, bound like a school prize, and given to me by my brother John. In the afternoon he went off by himself into the town and bought me from Dingley's, the popular haberdasher, a black serviceable rug, which has kept me warm in three continents and still holds its woof together.

My brother John came also to my bedside. He had received news of my sickness in Paris and had hurried to Sherborne. He would enter my room very early, before it was light, and we would discourse at large, I in a whisper, so as not to injure my lungs. And the early morning sounds of the ancient town would come in to us through the open windows—the almshouse bell, the convent bell, the crowing of cocks from distant back-yards.

As he left, one morning, for his breakfast at Acreman House, he met a beggar outside my door, and after his manner gave the rogue ten shillings. I observed the incident from my window and was full of indignation; reproaching him on his return to my room with many evil words. Was not I in the sorest need just then of everybody's money? What right had he to give so much to a lousy tramp with a great pack on his shoulders and a pair of stout legs under him?

My mother came to see me, that strange woman who ever loved sorrow rather than joy. She brought me flowers from the garden at home, little button chrysanthemums and a spray of arbutus berries from the tree in the laurel bushes leading down to the terrace walk. But my heart remained hard towards her. I knew that she resented my going to Switzerland and would have had me instead return quietly to Montacute to die peacefully there clinging to the Christian hope. And yet, how beautiful she could look sometimes, her face for a moment illuminated, that face which in its delicacy and refinement spoke of the inward life that her romantic spirit had been compelled to lead, as the wife of a man with the pride of a lion and the low forehead of a lion, and as the mother of eleven wilful and godless children.

Very different was my meeting with my brother Theodore, who came over from his hermitage at the other side of the County. His chief preoccupation seemed to be lest he himself should catch my complaint. He sat by the open window, inhaling the fresh air, and now and again drawing in his cheeks, as he uttered a thousand whimsical and fantastical observations. It was amusing to note the exaggerated deference he paid to the self-esteem of any schoolmaster who might come in, so that one who did not know would have thought that he prized nothing in the world more highly than the guinea-pig virtues of an English public-school man.

There also came to see me an old stone-mason from Montacute. He sat by my bedside, his whole demeanour displaying that particular exultation which one human being feels at seeing another caught in an evil trap. '*You have a Churchyard cough,*' he said. Now, his use of these words at once arrested my attention. Long after he had gone I could not get them out of my mind. They were like a draught from an ossuary. In a moment I had been vividly reminded of all the superstitious, uncouth usages which have gathered around death in an English village, usages which doubtless had their origin in the ever-recurring startled surprise of generations of simple human beings at seeing the grim transformation take place, usages begotten in long vigils at the sides of the dead, in white-washed chambers under thatched eaves, and manifesting themselves in such odd customs as putting white stockings on to cold feet, feet never again to tread down June grass, or break cat-ice on a December road. '*You have a Churchyard cough.*' These words, I say, fairly made me jump, bringing home to me, as they did, almost with the rigour of an epileptic fit, that it was I, and I alone, who, when all my dramatisations and sensationalisms were over, would be spending cold nights, cold years, cold centuries, alone in a cold elm-wood coffin.

CHAPTER TWO

A White Palace

THE SANATORIUM to which I was taken was one of those lofty and spacious hospitals which have sprung up during the last half-century, beyond all expectation, on the higher slopes of the Alps. And peculiar enough it looked, this ornate white palace, its southern side fretted with balconies as though with so many house-martins' nests. In truth, there must have been nearly a hundred such projections, each holding its own horizontal figure, swathed round and round in blankets, like a mummified bird imported from Egypt.

Night after night, when the moon, frail and luminous as the circular leaf of a silver poplar, rose high above the Frauenkirch valley, I would lean over my balustrade and look out across the sanatorium lawns, to where a group of larch trees stood casting ink-etched shadows on the snow, their slim stems and feathery twigs clearly visible in the universal nocturnal irradiation which at such hours envelops the Alps.

It was, indeed, a queer anomaly, this crew of sick people marooned on a mountain pass which for centuries had remained remote and unvisited by any except the hardiest peasants, men such as I would see on the Poste road in the daytime, bearded and smelling of cattle-dung. And at night, how these same bearded devils, with lungs of leather, would

15

fall to yodelling as they skimmed over the crisp snow, their bellies full of red wine, and with a ski on each heel! I would hear them and would sit up in my chair to peer out at the corner where the road turned to go down to Davos; and the sound of their goblin cries would echo along the hollow, hygienic corridors, echo up through the mountain forests, until it died away in the lonely reaches above the trees and in the windless spaces of the sparkling night sky. And yet, artificial and evil as our lot undoubtedly was, it could not have been called completely desperate. Most of us were still young. Was it this fact, or, as sometimes has been asserted, the very sickness from which we were suffering, that rendered us so daintily susceptible to the delights of love-making? I for one had been long a victim to those pernicious suppressions which, in many cases, give so lamentable a twist to the natures of young men who have suffered the very real disadvantage of having been born in the English middle classes, suppressions rendering them ungenerous and petty in their attitude to life, and, as Montaigne observed, 'tiresome and inconvenient in conversation'. I was therefor overjoyed to find myself in so fortunate a playground, and felt, in truth, the infinite content we might imagine experienced by a butterfly, a Red Admiral, let us say, which, after a weary flight across the asphalt streets of a city, suddenly finds itself in the happy seclusion of a garden full of geraniums and larkspur and salpiglossis and hot lavender. I differed, however, from many of my companions in that I passionately desired to live; and though I relished to the full the exceptionally civilised conditions within the sanatorium, yet, at the same time, I was reluctant to sacrifice any chance I might have of leaving it, cured of my disease, even for the most exceptional favours.

From November to March, I grew steadily better. By All Fools' Day my cough had stopped, and I appeared to be practically cured. If I had possessed enough wit, I would then and there have gathered up my belongings and departed for England. It was Doctor Huggard, the sagacious bald-headed Consul from Davos, who dissuaded me. 'You had better make sure of your cure,' he said. So that I, behaving for all the world like some yellow-striped wasp in this same garden we have spoken of, who, having crawled over his companions' backs to the very neck of the treacle-pot, incontinently turns again to dip his greedy nob into the precious sweetness at the bottom, arranged to stay on through the summer.

The thaw of the spring months had set in, and wide acres of ground had become green, revealing the fact that the dissolving layers of congealed snow on the hillsides had hidden fragile, exquisitely coloured petals pressing up from the chilled soil, and ready, when once they felt warmth and light, to convert the slopes of each mountainside into a Fra Angelico paradise. And the roe-deer, tired of scraping for fodder under the snow, tired of nibbling at grey-bearded lichen, came down from their winter retreats to graze on these open patches of fresh grass. And, lastly, the peasants emerged from the unventilated interiors of their log-houses, to dot the enormous landscape with their tiny figures. With the indefatigable, silent energy of ants they would scrape at the surface of their hillsides—men, women, and little children—and, when all was prepared, plant in symmetrical rows their store of last year's roots, preserved with so much care through the long cold months.

I would watch them at their work, sitting warm and happy under a granite rock, the smell of the freshly broken earth in my nostrils, that singular smell of the body of our planet which is the same in Africa, in America, in Europe.

By the end of the month of May, I suddenly became aware that my sickness had taken a turn for the worse. I recognised what had happened before any of the doctors. That particular taste in my mouth, surely it could mean nothing else! At first I was not alarmed. It seemed to me that I had only to be more strict with myself, only to concentrate my attention upon 'curing', and all would once more be well. By the end of June, however, I realised that I was far worse than I had ever been before. All the symptoms of the hideous complaint were once more showing themselves. Each afternoon, as the hours passed, I could feel my fever mounting higher and higher. I became languid and listless and very nervous. If at any time I fell asleep on my resting chair for a few moments, the wildest fantasies would course through my dreams, and I would wake to find myself bathed in a kind of death-dew, the fingers of my hands clammy as toadstools, the hair of my head drenched like seaweed. I could not conceive any possible escape from the predicament I was now in. A snare had been laid for me and I had run my head into the noose. A gin had been set for me and I had deliberately set my foot upon the pan. I could see before me nothing but perdition, nothing but to rot in the ground before ever I had properly understood what it was to be alive. My physical strength ebbed and ebbed, but not so the vital life-passion in me. I recoiled as violently from the thought of death as a pet rabbit from a lurcher dog. I looked wildly about for some respite, for some means by which I could postpone my doom. It seemed incredible to me that any one ever could become reconciled to dying. I would wake in the small hours of the morning, swaddled in fear. With scared eyes I would peer into the darkness of my room, and into the unknown days before me, and come to realise, during those tense, suspended moments, how completely unattended, how intolerably alone we are, each one of us, like cattle herded into a merciless stockyard, to be driven into the shambles, separately, when our turn comes.

Even now that my mind is no longer as tender as it was then, even now that I have become more philosophical and more accustomed to out-face the worst, I often find myself suspecting that it is only very rarely that even the most clear-sighted of us grasp the actual terms of our existence, each tremulous, intellectual soul being set shockingly apart, to endure as best it may its own destruction.

For hours and hours I lay supine, looking at the glass door opening on to my balcony, that door which at night took to itself something of the pallor of a linen shroud, hung up on a clothes-line, looking at it with the same hopeless expression that I was to see long afterwards in the eyes of a cat, whose spine had been broken and who was awaiting a final blow from my hand as it lay on the verandah of an African farm. Very slowly the days passed. I would spend whole afternoons watching the sunlight on the mountain above the Frauenkïrch village. Outlined sharply against the sky, its uneven topmost ridge limned the prostrate figure of a woman. There she lay, through winter, through summer, in her winding-sheet of snow, her head, her paps, her knees, her feet, clearly visible. This mass of primeval, recumbent granite was called by the Swiss peasants, 'Die tote Königin', the dead Queen, but at the English table it was always referred to, with the unerring faculty of the British for coining phrases that bear upon them, like their own heavy round pennies, the stamp of the island taste, as 'Queen Victoria in Bed'.

And then, one July midnight, a blood-vessel broke. I waked suddenly to feel that insufferable bubbling sensation in my chest, so familiar to consumptives. There was a rush of blood. I coughed and gasped for breath. Presently, with the pretty egotism of youth, I dipped my fountain-pen into the basin at my bedside and scratched a red cross on my diary, a cross such as a tramp might have made who could not sign his name, and yet who wished to record some important event in his wayfaring.

All night I lay on my back, scarcely daring to move. The sanatorium doctors stood by my bedside. They injected me with gelatine. They exhorted me to remain motionless. Eventually, however, they were called away to attend upon a young English boy named Burton, who had also been taken ill on this same Sunday night. His room was opposite mine,

20

and as I lay I could hear him giving those short, choking coughs that are so unmistakable. At intervals I would answer him in the same manner from my side of the long, narrow white-enamelled corridor, which smelt of disinfectants, and whose audible silence at night would be disturbed by no other noise than the occasional opening and shutting of a well-hung door. As the hours passed, the saltish, sticky taste of the blood became horrible to me. I shook as a young colt might which has been down on a frozen road and is apprehensive of another fall.

The dawn came at last. Gradually the forlorn whiteness of the blank panes grew more and more apparent, until I was able to watch the movements of a moth fluttering and fluttering down the inexplicable, transparent barrier which lay between its weary wings and freedom, a transparent barrier spotted over with infinitesimal heaps of white excrement left there by countless house-flies already imprisoned hopelessly in Room 57, on *Etage* 3.

CHAPTER THREE

Out of the Pit

VERY SLOWLY, as the weeks went by, my fever abated. It was a long time, however, before I was able to get out of bed. When I tried to stand, with the red-haired man-servant, Carl, supporting me, I found that my legs bent under my weight like limp straws. Doctor Huggard sounded me. 'I think you have got through this fairly well, but many things may happen before you recover,' observed the cautious old man, whose head was as bare as the egg of an ostrich, and who himself was to be underground before the year was out. For months I lay on my back, doing little but watch from morning till evening the play of light upon the high precipices of the dead Queen.

By the beginning of December, I was strong enough to come downstairs. But even so I was terrified of a second hæmorrhage. After the slightest exertion I would feel my chest aching and my temperature rising. I was now determined to get well. I would content myself with stepping silently through the lofty vestibule; for beauty, being satisfied with looking at the cyclamen and azaleas which stood in pots by the window. When I did say a few words, it was to my friend Wilbraham, or to the philosophic Hungarian, rather than to Betty, Aida, or Zenäide. At this time I was as timid as a brown hare. I developed the habit of pressing the fingers of my left hand against that part of my chest which I knew to be badly affected, as though by so simple a means to avert any fresh catastrophe. This absurd form of neurosis cost me two waistcoats; the constant pressure of my fingers gradually wearing a hole through them.

A sudden change in the weather would be sufficient to send me up to my chamber. Sick with fear, I would creep back to bed without any orders from the doctor, and lie there listening to the wind that had suddenly got up and that was making the red striped awning of my balcony rattle, overturning, with a bang and the sound of dripping water, the vase of flowers I had forgotten to bring in from the little table by my chair.

The presence of Wilbraham in the sanatorium came to be a great source of consolation to me; and this in spite of the fact that he would do all in his power to bring my wild extravagances into the correct moderation of the scholar and the gentleman. I remember once talking in my enthusiastic manner about the West of England. I described Sedgemoor to him and how it looks on an autumn afternoon, with its pollard willows appearing like troops of old women coming back from Middlezoy market with baskets on their heads. I described Ilchester to him and told him how pleasantly the Fosse Way leads you down from Tintinhull on a fine spring evening, with pickerel flowers coming out in the ditches, and with the lilac blossoms in the cottage garden at the top of Hunger Hill casting spiral shadows upon the first white dust of the old Roman road. I also spoke of the river Parret and how it winds through a hundred freehold orchards, which in the month of May scatter rose-tinted petals on its cider-coloured, slowly moving waters full of doltish, red-finned roach. To all this Wilbraham answered, raising his aristocratic head, which had already become so dear to me, 'Somerset is an historical county, a recognised historical county.'

I recall, too, how astonished he was, and how amused, when I came to him one evening in high excitement at having been shown by a German boy a certain treasured heirloom brought with him to the sanatorium and kept always at his bedside, nothing less, in fact, than a wooden salad spoon that had once belonged to Wolfgang Goethe. The sight of this simple piece of wood had thrilled my imagination. It was the first object of the physical world which had connected me with the great man, and actually to handle the very instrument used by Goethe for stirring his cresses was to me a most rare and noble experience.

I used to have the strangest dreams at this time of convalescence. Especially would I dream about death. I had done this since my childhood, but during this period these insubstantial images would be more palpable, more real, than ever before. I would be wandering over some obscure dream-landscape, when I would become suddenly aware of a certain smell assailing my nostrils. It would be sweet and at the same time foul. 'Ha!' I would say to myself, 'the smell of mortality, the smell of decaying human flesh!' And immediately the ground upon which I was standing would sink under me and I would find myself struggling in a graveyard

which was giving way in all directions, struggling like a
horse in a Wyoming 'soap-hole', with the mould everywhere crumbling and rotting boards breaking through into
I knew not what horrors! And I discovered, in after-years,
on occasions when I have approached with too much confidence the corpses of those I have loved, that the smell
of my dreams *was* the smell of dead human bodies, a
smell subtly different from that which rises from dead
cattle.

The nurse one day told me that a little lady on the second
floor, who had been sick for many years, had asked if I
would come and visit her. I went to her room. Never in
my life had I seen anybody so fragile. It was like talking to
gossamer, talking to a dandelion-seed. One felt that the
very steam from her coffee-pot at her bedside might well
be sufficient to waft her away, out of the window and over
the cold mountains. To be able to retain one's poise to the
end, to be able to die beautifully, that in itself is an achievement. 'The nurse, after staying with me ten minutes,
always says, "I must go now to Mr. Powys".' I wish I could
convey how pretty, how provocative the little lady looked
as she spoke these words. I went back to my room thinking
that the only unpardonable sins are those committed in an
unimaginative mood. It is more cursed to be dull and obtuse
and unperceptive of other people's feelings than to indulge
to the uttermost one's most frolicsome fancies. Insensitive-
ness is the one cardinal sin.

It was a desolate afternoon. A gusty wind was blowing,
carrying with it at intervals particles of snow dislodged

from the projecting wooden cornices of balconies above mine. Two charwomen were busy cleaning the empty room next door. The sound of their damp mops flopping on the linoleum, the sound of their dispirited servant voices, as they reached my ears from out that garnished mausoleum, filled my soul with a devastating melancholy. It was not till the evening that I took heart again, and this because of a letter from my brother Willie, who had been shooting snipe in the water-meadows of his farm in Somerset. He enclosed a beak of a snipe in his letter. 'Hulloa,' says he, 'here's a girt beak very near long enough to reach from me to you.'

One day, before lunch, I dared to talk with Daphne, who looked as mischievous and enticing as ever. Against all prudence I persuaded her to come up with me to my rooms. She scanned the volumes in my poor library. 'Have you any naughty books?' she asked.

That evening the sun went down in splendour. At first, a line of clouds above the mountain became transformed into gold, then transformed into orange, then into red, then into crimson, into scarlet! 'See where Christ's blood streams in the firmament!' And between the colour-splashed clouds there lay the clear, green light of Eternity. I was sure of it. I cried out to God. And then, across the Frauenkirch valley, across the river whose snow-banks are hollowed out by lukewarm sewage from Davos Platz, a belated blackbird flew, croaking to itself.

After dinner, Wilbraham brought in a poem dedicated to me. It began:

> *Lately in Platonic mood*
> *I expressed the judgement crude*
> *That a man of taste must find*
> *Caresses of the eye and mind*
> *Than the touch of those that are*
> *Of the senses finer far :*
> *But my fairy Zenäide*
> *Faithful of another creed*
> *Yester 'eve constrainèd me*
> *To recant this heresy*
> . . . .

I read to him extracts from Louis Wilkinson's letter referring to 'the Great O.B.' having been sacked from Cambridge. 'What a disgraceful business! These academic mediocrities, these yellow-blooded sneaking P——s and R——s yelping at the heels of the old man in currish concert to drive him out—the only figure of distinction, the only individual.' He had heard from the O.B. himself, who described the affair 'as the most scandalous tissue of intrigue and treachery that ever stained the annals of the University'. Louis also wrote that he had heard from John. 'Do you remember how Lulu always spoke of *the* Broadway, instead of simply Broadway, and what a queer fluffiness and lazy, blurred leisureliness that simple prefix evoked?'

Just before twelve o'clock, on the last night of the year, Wilbraham asked me three questions.

'Is Christianity true?'

'*No, Christianity is not true.*'
'Is there a God?'
'*No, there is no God.*'
'Is there life after death?'
'*No, there is no life after death.*'

Presently I rose, and shutting the door upon the close, crowded room where we had been sitting, stepped out into the night. I walked to the further end of the empty verandah, long as a gallery, and stood for a moment regarding the white slopes about me. Suddenly there came to my ears, echoing up the mountain valley, the happy, unaffrighted music of church bells. Already, I thought, it is the morning of the New Year.

CHAPTER FOUR

'Virginibus Puerisque'

Howewer much one's own emotions may be involved by what one experiences, however much one's own intellect may become implicated in the spectacle of existence, one must on no account forget the simple philosophic axiom that 'NOTHING MATTERS'. Thus I thought as I lay on my *Lieger* chair, watching the soft snowflakes dancing past my balcony, wavering, hesitating, fluttering down, each to its destined resting-place. I was eating a couple of blue trout. With punctilious care I extracted with the prongs of my fork their round white eye-balls. Very early in life I had made the discovery that in the rotund retinas of a fish's goggle eyes are retained its very quintessential juices. 'One's code of morality should be merely an affair of good manners and expedience.'

And yet how infinitely piteous, how infinitely grievous a thing life can sometimes seem! I am thinking now of the look in the eyes of a girl from Cornwall, left here yesterday by her aunt, and who this morning was ruefully watching a row of icicles dripping on to the wooden floor of the verandah near her chair. 'I am very bad and very lonely,' she told me. 'I should not mind so much if only I had my dogs with me.' I went up to my room. On the table at the end of the white *étage* they had set a fresh assortment of

flowers. There were some hyacinths exquisitely fragrant in
a transmuted ray of sunshine, which fell on them through
a double glass window. As I stopped, I was transported in
a single instant to the top lawn at Montacute, where, in
the round bed near the acacia, opposite the drawing-room
window, Rogers used to plant bulbs capable in the lovely
spring sunshine of sprouting and burgeoning into just such
splendid blossoms. As I turned away, I was called into the
German boy's room. The wooden spoon was still at his
bedside. We talked together. 'You then regard God as little
better than a fool?' 'Yes; but He has time to learn; we have
not.' I touched his hand. 'Oh, I am *kaput*,' he murmured,
and with tears in his eyes turned his face to the wall. I had
been told that he had already published a book, and I made
some allusion to it. 'No,' he said, 'I have done nothing but
try to cure this'—and he tapped his chest—'and even that
has been a failure.' We spoke of Christianity. 'What if the
God whom the Jews caught trespassing and nailed to the
cross had been a young girl instead of a young man? What
if an only beloved daughter had been given as a perfect and
sufficient sacrifice?' 'EIN MADCHEN AM KREUTZE,' repeated
the boy, as though pleased by the fantastical conceit. 'There
may be,' I said, 'more in this matter than we think. Who
knows but Jesus really *was* an inspired and magnanimous
goblin, born of a goblin sire and of a goblin dam, in a hidden
grotto, under a cactus tree, somewhere above the River
Jordan?' The boy is learning to play the guitar in anticipa-
tion of his last days. 'You can play it in bed, which you cannot do with a piano,' he explained. I left him nursing the

instrument and filling the room with a sweet melody, his slender fingers moving to and fro, and his body swaying in harmony with the music, like a horned poppy on the edge of a precipice. He might have been taken, I thought, as a symbolic figure celebrating the last hours of the departing senses. After lunch I visited Wilbraham's room, and from his window we witnessed the departure of Miss Appleyard. It was a sombre sight. Supported on one side by Mrs. St. John and on the other by a nurse, she trod down the white steps with the stiff ineptitude of a cadaver.

As I returned from my walk that afternoon I came across a bundle of hay left in the snow by the side of the road. It smelt the same as meadow-hay at home, and when I examined it closely I could see remnants of crushed, dried-up flowers, but how disconsolate it looked against this ever-lasting white background! I found letters waiting for me when I got back. One was from John. He said he had heard from Willie. 'Is there anything except the soil, the earth, the blessed dung of cart-horses and pigs, that really conveys health into the veins of mortal men? I fancy that the old fellow has never known Fear, the Grey Rider, the lonely Kite flying over the sands, the shadowy finger pointing to the unknown dread, to the imminent and yet indescribable calamity—No, the divine oblivion of cider and ditch-digging, of making bulls leap cows, and bringing foals into the light of day, drives all abnormal terror from that Praxitilean forehead of sweet curls. . . . O Lulu, I am so tired. I long to drink rest as a traveller in the desert might kneel down and put his face to a palm-shadowed well.' There was also a letter from Theodore. 'So, old friend, let your head rest at ease, let your old mind hug itself, seeing that you will again walk soon. Remember old Gammer Guffle, of this town, who was in bed fifty years, and then got him up and walked, and Corporal Cutflesh, who is drunk five days in a week with bullets in his body as many as peas in a pod. You will return to pick up shells and cull yellow seaweed, old rogue, honest companion. Farewell. Theodore.'

In the evening I looked nervously at myself in the glass. Was I growing thinner? This suspicion set me brooding upon the destined history of each of our bodies: how they grow heavier and heavier, until they touch the maximum weight ordained for them in their life, and then grow lighter and lighter, until finally what is left of them in churchyard mould would scarcely offset a pound of raisins on a pair of kitchen scales. Coming in one day, from my walk, I met the Hungarian. 'Are you living or dying?' he asked. 'Living,' I asseverated stoutly. 'Damn!' he snapped, doubtless suspecting that I spoke truth. 'All wise men,' he went on, 'are pessimists. The only thing for us to do is to work day and night, so as to forget our destiny.' I left him and went and sat with Daphne for a little. 'I could not endure that you should be wicked with any one but me.'

Gradually the weeks passed until once more there were indications that the snow was beginning to melt. By the end of March I was again taking long walks. I even went as far as the old white mill, where the road turns down to the Frauenkirch. By climbing over a dissolving, discoloured snowdrift, into which I sank nearly up to my knees, I actually touched the rough surface of its wall, so that I might mark this stage in my recovery, placing my finger on a certain brown area, where the plaster had fallen away, and which had the shape, so it seemed to me, of a dromedary. I spent half an hour in front of the mill, seated on a pile of resin-scented pine logs. Presently a peasant leading a mouse-coloured cow, stopped for a drink of red wine. His host came out and stood with him. As I watched them grouped thus before me, so close that I could sometimes feel the moist breath of the animal, I seemed to undergo a kind of mystical revelation as to the reality of concrete life. I became vividly aware of the actual moment, of the cow with its docile, brown eye, of the genial, bearded peasants, of the cup of red, bitter-tasting wine, as if sublimated in some curious way against that eternity of white and blue. Over the snow at my feet a shivering black fly crept, struggling to free each minute hairy foot from the ghastly white waste on which it had settled. I wanted to come to its assistance; but just as I moved, thinking I might persuade it to walk upon my alpenstock, the cow also moved, and an indifferent, cloven hoof carried the persevering insect down into an inch-deep hole of hopeless perdition.

On the way back, near the large châlet, where the three hams hang in the window, I met Watson, who told me that the Cornish girl had just had a hæmorrhage. So, all that last night, as I was talking to her about Dartmoor, the sickness was working its evil under her silk blouse! I happened to go up the lift with the white-coated German doctor, and took the opportunity of asking how she was. 'Not very well just now.' 'She hasn't been ill again to-day, has she?' 'Yes, she has.' And with these three words in my ears I stepped out upon the landing of the Third Floor.

In the evening the 'decadent' sat with me on my balcony. 'There must be a purpose, a meaning, somewhere in the universe,' he said. 'I would shoot myself if I thought it was not so.'—'But why shoot yourself? Surely for an intrepid mind there is something exciting, exhilarating, about the idea of an aimless, irresponsible universe, a Gothic universe?'

When he left I settled myself to try to read that courtly Collect, 'Virginibus Puerisque', written at Davos Platz thirty years ago. In a little while there came a knock at my door and Daphne entered. She looked radiant. She, at any rate, will get quite well again. 'Why are your eyes so large and deep to-night, Daphne?' I asked. 'Because of love, because of love,' lightly she laughed.

CHAPTER FIVE

A Home-coming

B Y THE end of April I was strong enough to travel,
and my brother John came out to Davos Platz to
fetch me home. I recollect standing by his side
in the main thoroughfare of the town while he looked about
him in dismay at the rows of horizontal figures lying in drab
balconies on each side of the street. 'Ech!' he exclaimed,
'that we might see Jesus walking through these streets,
followed a little way behind by his disciples, bearded,
venerable, and discussing some nice theological point.'

We reached Folkestone on May Day, and were soon at
Montacute. My proud sister Gertrude, with tender care,
had prepared the nursery for me, setting my bed by the
window, which looked out upon the twisted boughs of the
acacia, boughs whose particular twists and turns were as
familiar to me as my own knuckle and knee joints. The
nursery had always been one of the pleasantest rooms in the
house, so much more sunny and cheerful than the small
chamber at the end of the north wing, where, as boys, we
used to sleep, and which was known as the 'end room',
and was always regarded as damp by my mother, who would
be careful to see that our woollen vests were carried down
to the kitchen fire each Saturday night, so that 'the chill of
the end room' would be out of them when we dressed on
Sunday morning.

From the nursery window I could see, through the trees, like a miniature engraving, a view of the Abbey. I also looked out upon a line of Wellingtonias in the field opposite, cone-shaped tapering trees, whose forms, so neatly symmetrical, had always struck us children as being the exact replicas of the trees which we were constantly arranging on the table, together with tiny, unsteady, unpainted animals. A deodar grew at the top of the Montacute House drive, and I could watch the particular branch which, as a child, had so fascinated me, because, in outline against a patch of sky to the left of the Abbey, it would take to itself the shape of a rider on horseback. How often on a late October afternoon, when our nurse, Emily Clare, was seated on the horsehair sofa sewing, and we were waiting for the lamp to be brought in by the maid, had I not gone across to this very window to look out at the swaying movements of the imaginary rider, while far above him, far above the pointed tree of which he was a part, far above the topmost buttress of the Abbey gateway a myriad rooks would sweep across the sky, like black leaves tossed this way and that by the wild autumnal wind! This in winter. In summer the prospect would be entirely altered. Muffled up in folds upon folds of clematis, the window would then look out upon a lawn thick-grown with heavy flowers, the acacia itself, even, each year, to one's utter amazement, producing out of its apparently dead wood a profusion of creamy-white blossoms, smelling, if crushed in the hand, not unlike the everlasting sweet-peas which grew outside the tool-house window.

At first I did not dare to walk far. What a delight to be back again in these fields and lanes where one's spirit, no less than one's eyes, could be restored by the colour of green! And how sensitive I was after my long exile in the mountains, how sensitive to the richness of these lowland meadows, where under each field-hedge golden-billed cock blackbirds stepped about in the cool grass, as much at ease as in a garden!

One morning found me walking with John to Stoke churchyard. We had been here often in the old days. We liked to look at the ancient tympanum of Ham stone above the church door. Though coated with the green mildew of the centuries, it represented still quite clearly King Stephen shooting an arrow at his rival, the granddaughter of the Conqueror, chipped out by the old mason in the form of a retreating lioness. The enormous stone had been carved and put into place when King Stephen still sat upon the throne of England.

We found that there were workmen in the churchyard occupied in raising the mediæval village cross which for as long as I could remember had been lying amongst the nettles under the churchyard wall, and which now, thanks to the energy of the parish priest, was to be set upright once more on this bright summer morning. A firm base had been prepared for it, and it seemed likely, when once it was placed in its new position, that it would be able to weather as many winters as the door-head which marked in so dramatic a way the zodiac-sign of the Norman King, dead so long ago. 'To appreciate the beauty and pathos of Christi-

one must not believe too much,' John remarked.
an amazing episode in the history of humanity is the
rance of this cult! How wonderful, and yet how in-
essibly melancholy!' We watched the men hoisting
the monolith. Their trousers—made yellow by the dust of
Ham stone—were brushing against some crimson roses
which grew near the path. 'It is equally strange to think,' I
said, 'that when that cross falls again from its upright position
Christianity will be dead as earth.'

We walked up the little lane behind. Several plants of
Herb Robert were growing in the crumbling interstices of
the churchyard wall. I picked some and went on my way,
over the dry spring mould of the lane, alternately crushing
them and smelling them. The herbage of the banks above
the ditches, on both sides of the lane rose up until they
merged with the light-green leaves, each edged with a
delicate silver down, of the beech trees growing in the two
hedgerows. 'There is no excuse for ennui and weariness,'
said John. 'How mad in this world to take anything for
granted! The thing to do is to divert your mind from what
is mean and sordid, so that large, luminous thoughts may
roll in upon it like amber-coloured waves.'

At the top of the lane we met Fred Chant. 'Well, I'll be
damned!' he exclaimed. 'I never looked to see ye back,
Master Llewelyn, 'cept as a corpse, if ye do follow my
meaning.' While we stood talking, I kept looking at a gorse
bush, heavily scented, embossed with golden bloom, about
which there buzzed a bee with two brown honey-bags on
its thighs and a murmuring rapture in its heart. The old

wood-cutter looked me up and down, from the hat on my head to the boots on my feet, stained yellow with buttercup-dust. 'Ye may linger out the summer,' he said judiciously; 'but you'll never get rid of that cough. These here doctors say they can cure ye, but they cannot do it. They can patch ye up, maybe, but, never fear, you'll soon be a-wearing a green coat.' By 'wearing a green coat', he referred, I knew, to the green grass, which he was convinced would soon be growing over my grave. We walked on through the wood. 'I am afraid I have the same kind of sneaking desire for some sort of metaphysical theory as a background to life that others have for a definite religion,' remarked John, as we approached the gate into Hedgecock. 'Is not a vivid apprehension of life's brevity sufficient?' I asked him.

That night a barn-door owl waked me with its hooting. It had settled on the acacia, on the bough nearest my window, on the bough with the iron clamp about it. 'Dead feet! Dead feet!' it called. I could see its broad humped form quite clearly against the night sky, and I could not but envy it its long still hours in the deserted garden, alone with the smokeless summer chimneys, with the gleaming slate roofs, with the haunted, whispering trees, and with the silent carriage-drive lying like a frozen river between black lawns.

The Phelips family were away that year, but they gave me leave to walk in their garden as much as I liked. And so, when I became tired of our own terrace walk, I would cross the orchard by the old ruined house, and presently be wandering in the stately pleasure-grounds of the famous Elizabethan mansion. I would find it hard to indicate how

deeply I was influenced by the seclusion and patrician
dignity of those fine walks, with their tall yew hedges, and
with their wide spaces of sun-baked garden masonry, which
seemed to exhale, during each noontide recalescence of
that cloudless summer, a heat of their own, altogether
different from the heat which rose from the mown lawns,
the short-cropped turf of which would feel to my hand,
when I knelt down to touch it, like a live pelt.

I would spend hours and hours at the end of the Cedar
Piece, looking at the daisies, at the narcissi, at the yellow
tulips, at a bullfinch with a beautiful cherry-coloured breast
hopping about amongst the green fir-cones; or gazing off
into the park, through an atmosphere quivering, palpitating,
instinct with life, to where the heavy shadows of the great
elms fell upon the pasture-grass like pools of deep water;
and then suddenly from some unseen retreat in that favoured
pleasaunce, so that I listened in a kind of ecstasy, a painted
peacock would scream out to God its shrill, fantastic,
acquiescence.

Only once was my happiness in any way disturbed in
those gardens. I had been sitting on the steps outside the
old stone pigeon-house, listening to the drowsy cooing that
came from its hollow interior, where in an atmosphere of
feathers and doves' excrement, innumerable fan-tailed
pigeons sat dozing away the long afternoon, when suddenly
I caught sight of the figure of a neighbouring clergyman
coming towards me. I had no time to slip away. I knew him
to be a tiresome young man, full of zeal. I uttered a few
civil words and then indicated as best I was able that I

considered it time for our chance encounter to end. He would not budge. I looked into his pin-point eyes, eager and preoccupied as those of some damned fanatical black cat on its way to save its kittens from a burning barn. Presently it dawned on me that he had some especial communication to make. I was filled with alarm. Proximity to such an individual in such a place was extremely distasteful. He was the kind of person who should never have been allowed to enter so beautiful a garden, who should have been turned away by Mr. Jack Hull at the lodge gates.

But what was he going to say? Apparently some young village boy of his parish had spoken to him of me, had used me, in fact, as evidence to support his own freethinking views, asserting that there surely could be no good God directing the affairs of the world when a young man as innocent of sin as myself was struck down with a fatal illness. At first I listened to his tale with amusement. Then when I found that he was suggesting that I should walk over myself and reason with the young infidel, my attitude changed. 'I could not possibly do such a thing,' I hurriedly assured him. 'After all,' I added, by way of detaching myself completely from the man, 'I, too, am something of a latitudinarian.' 'What is your great difficulty? The incarnation?' I doffed my hat and ran. Coming up through the lower orchard, I disturbed a rabbit, which raced away and sprang into the hedge by the old lane. I watched a bramble, disturbed by its furry belly in its last jump, tremble for a few seconds before resuming its accustomed stillness under that ocean of sweet blossoms.

CHAPTER SIX

The King's Affairs

IT WAS during the early part of this summer that Louis Wilkinson came to stay with me. In appearance he seemed exactly the same as in the old days at Cambridge. He was full of good talk. He told me that he had the distinction of being the first person to write to Oscar Wilde sympathetically after his conviction. We were strolling through the fields below Batemore when he made this remark, and presently we came to the wishing-well, where we sat for a while. 'What do y'lack? What do y'lack?' croaked a bullfrog, with a voice bass as the lowing of an ox, asquat on the edge of the crystal pool under a hart's-tongue fern. 'Long life, give me long life,' I cried.

Theodore paid us a visit one day. We went a walk together, all four of us, but John could not go far, because he had a bad toe. He wore an enormous moccasin and came limping after us like an injured cacodæmon. We sat on a seat in Park Covert. Louis was stung by a nettle. Cursing with surprise and rage, he stamped it deep into the ground, together with many pink-campions. It was done before John had time to interfere. We walked on up the moss-grown, velvet path. 'Which of us three would you prefer to be God?' asked John. 'Louis,' I said, 'because he is so moral and just.' 'Good heavens,' John answered; 'but think of his antipathy for nature. Why, he'd make the world of boulevards; and between them would lay blank, impenetrable, palpable voids; where now is nature there would be great belching spaces of roaring chaos.' Before lunch we sat in the terrace walk. 'I feel,' said Theodore, drawing in his cheeks, 'like Southey in Portugal.' I think he enjoyed himself, however, for three days later my mother received this letter from him: 'My dear Mother, I enjoyed seeing you very much. I was sorry Jack had a bad toe, but if he had had a well toe he might have fallen into a mire or evil place. Theodore.' A letter came to me from Louis by the same post. 'I shall bathe in the recollection of last week's golden hours. My egoism *is* adamantine, but I swear, dearest Lulu, I love you, even though I drink champagne over your death-bed. Who knows but you will drink over mine? You shall not die, but live. Yours is the star of the morning. A hundred thousand embraces await you in the arms of unborn to-morrows, and amorous kisses without count.'

Early in the summer I visited Pit Pond. This deep, black pond, lying in the heart of Pit Wood, had a thousand memories for me. As children, we used to skate on it, waiting impatiently, whenever there was a spell of cold weather, 'for Pitt Pond to bear'. On many occasions have I seen my father sail round the miniature island in its centre with enormous, swift-gliding strides. Because he himself could not do figure-skating he had the greatest contempt for it, and left us all with the lifelong impression that to be able to swoop round and round a pond in rapid circles was incomparably a finer achievement than to cut any number of eights on the ice. 'I never cared much for fancy skating,'

he would say, coming up to the bank where Littleton,
always competent and always unselfish in such matters, was
on his knees, adjusting my sister Marian's skates; and away
he would go again, round and round and round, sending
great, far-reaching, resonant cracks up under the boat-
house, where a pleasure-boat was still lying, its keel held
fast in frozen mud—mud, which, when it thawed,
smelt of the skeletons of eels, and yet contained in its black
ooze rough oyster-shells with mother-of-pearl interiors of
unparalleled smoothness and beauty.

Those brief periods of frosty weather were always
thrilling. Even at midday, when one was returning to a
lunch of cold beef and walnut pickles (pickles made of the
very same walnuts, black and wrinkled, that I had seen laid
out on a tray in the sun, in front of the kitchen window,
with frugal foresight, while it was still summer), particles
of hoar frost would yet remain intact wherever there was
shadow, and even where there was no shadow, though the
surface of the ground would be soft, one would be able still
to feel 'the bone' in it. And after what a strange manner
one's childish fancy used to be provoked by looking down
through the black ice of Pitt Pond to see a fish deep-embedded
in the transparent substance, a fish perfectly preserved,
like an ornament in glass, caught obviously unawares as it
loitered too long near the surface on the first evening
when our weather-vane above the 'end room' had swung
suddenly round to the north-east.

As I approached the pond on this particular morning, I
found it difficult to believe that winter winds could ever

strip bare the foliage-encysted branches of the great oak trees which stood about the deserted keeper's cottage, each separate, irregular, pendent leaf being of so rich and of so deep a green. I was alone. Everybody had gone to church. I advanced along the path by the laurels. A rabbit with broken back rolled out of my way. It tumbled into a bed of nettles, but I had plenty of time to see the agonised look that its brown eyes gave me. A cuckoo kept bawling from the direction of Park Mill. A brown mallard piloted her brood across the shadowed level of the pond. Dragonflies were hovering everywhere, sometimes darting over the water, sometimes returning to poise themselves like slender shafts of blue and red enamel on the purple-tinted water-mint. When I reached the deep end of the pond I paused and looked into the water. Countless round beetles were paddling about below its surface, now and again turning turtle and exposing their white bellies. A swan near 'the island' uttered sharp, unexpected, springtime cries.

From the unseen incorrigible cuckoo, from the lascivious swan, from the adroitly steering duck, from the superficial dragonflies, and from these jolly sportive beetles, turning themselves, arse over tip, so gravely under water, I learnt the truth of the Pantagruelian aphorism, 'Do what thou wilt.' 'Fay que ce vouldray.' 'But what of the rabbit? Could you not so much as step out of your way to crack its skull with your ash plant?' murmured a spirit.

That evening my mother came and read to me in the terrace walk. She read Walt Whitman.

What blab is this about vice and virtue?
Evil propels me and the reform of evil propels me;
I stand indifferent.

My mother was one who ever preferred the shady side of the road, and would rather carry in her hand a white foxglove than a coloured foxglove. When she was tired of reading we walked together in the orchard. The last rays of the sun slanting through the beech trees slapped the flank of a great sow and transfigured it. 'So the spirit of God will light up the most degraded soul,' said my mother. The orchard looked strange and unreal in the tempered light, as though it were under water. She said she felt ill. 'I want like an animal to hide myself, to crawl into a hole, into a bush.' We came back, to hear the voice of my father as he walked through the potato garden in the cool of the evening. And it sounded in my ears as natural as any of the familiar sounds that used to make up our daily life, as natural as the slam of the back gate, as the ringing of the outside bell, calling us into the schoolroom from our play. At family prayers in the evening he prayed that we should not be won over by 'seducing words', but should instead live in 'purity and holiness as before God'. How could I feel anything but a deep affection for him as he knelt there on Uncle Littleton's tiger-skin, with his elbows to the left of the silver inkstand and to the right of my mother's Moxon edition of Tennyson's poems? As for his intellectual notions, that's another matter. Those family prayers were in truth something to remember. Punctually at ten o'clock each evening, my father would turn to my mother and say, 'I think we might ring now for the maidens.' I can well recall how that last word caused Louis Wilkinson to prick up his ears, when he heard it uttered the first time, and how crestfallen he looked when there entered, one behind the other, the four faithful servants who had been in the house as long as I could remember.

Very noble my father appeared on Coronation Day, as he marched at the head of the procession through the village, several inches taller than anybody else, in full canonical dress. And what a gentleman the old man looked, as he stood in the Park, his bared white head clear-cut against the foliage of an elm! I tried to imprint the scene upon my memory. The day had begun badly, with mist. 'What is King George doing now?' questioned John at breakfast. 'Fussing in and out, and tapping *his* barometer?'

In the afternoon we went for a walk through Park Covert. How exquisite the foxgloves with their silken, spotted throats! I got into trouble for carelessly crushing one of them as we rested at the top of the path. 'Life of any kind, however undeveloped, should be regarded,' John said. 'We ought, each one of us, to be aware of the separate individual life of every bit of weed, of every variety of existence around us.' At night I looked out of the 'end room' window and saw several hundred bonfires in celebration of the King's affairs. I could see a light on Dunkery Beacon, on Camelot, on Pilsdon, on the Quantocks, and on Wynyard's Gap.

The next day I walked by myself to Park Mill, some three

miles out of Montacute, over the fields. I had often walked to the cottages there with my father. In the nearest of them used to live three silent women, like the Three Fates. One of these women was rumoured to have once had a sailor lover. The atmosphere of the room in which these three silent sisters sat, eking out a bare existence by making gloves, was intense with deep, smouldering passions. Even as a child I used to wonder what thoughts were revolving in those large, melancholy, animal heads, which day after day, year after year, looked out of the same small window. They would place a chair for my father, and there he would sit, apparently unperturbed by that listening silence, and after a while, when an appropriate interval would seem to have elapsed, he would fumble in his purse for half-a-crown, and take his departure. And on our way back, my father's spirits would rise. Perhaps he was thinking of the steaming tea waiting for him, and the warmth and friendliness of his dining-room, with his wife at one end of the long table and his eleven children about him; for as soon as we came out on to Batemore and saw the village lights below us, he would have an ecstasy, and stride forward, rubbing his hands together, as any one of his six sons will do to this day, when they become aware from time to time of the simple satisfaction of being above ground.

The Three Fates had gone now. Doubtless they had been dug into yellow clay by the Montacute sacristan. Sammy Guard and his ramshackle family were installed in their cottage. I stopped to talk with them for a few moments. The eldest girl, Lotty, came out and stood playing with a brindled gib-cat. The mother told me that the girl sleeps in the room overlooking Pit Wood. The glass was out of her window. It must be wild and rough sleeping there in the winter, with owls in the cold trees answering the husky bark of vixen-foxes. And during these summer months how the bats must flutter in and out over the girl's sleeping head! Old Sam Guard himself came in before I had left. He had been cutting a hedge near the withy bed. 'I've got a tidy toy up there,' I heard him say. 'Goo-o-o. Why, they thorns be as big round as elms. I be b—— some of 'em be twisters.'

CHAPTER SEVEN

August

THAT SUMMER was the hottest I have ever known in England. Day after day the sun rose over the horizon behind Vag farm into a cloudless sky. The pastures were no longer green. The cattle roamed over the brown grass-fields like famished eland on diminutive, scorched-up African veldts. There was so little water flowing in the deep river-bed of the Yeo that it was possible at almost any point in its long, winding course to paddle across it. The chub, fearful of being stranded in shallow water, kept themselves at the bottom of the few deep holes that remained. The stock spent long hours in standing about in places where the river was shaded by a group of alders, by an oak tree, or by the stonework of some old bridge. The grasshoppers skipped from bent to bent, the butterflies from flower-head to flower-head. The crust of the earth cracked and cracked, so that I was often able, right out in the middle of a field, to put my walking-stick into a crevice two or three feet deep. Many farmers were compelled to cut down saplings from the hedges, and branches from the trees, to save their cattle from starving. Not one of them but was short of 'keep'. As each Friday they came back from Yeovil market, they would do nothing but lament about the state of the country, as seen in panoramic view through the open window of a third-class railway-carriage.

On the hottest of all the days of that summer, when, as we learnt afterwards, the thermometer stood at one hundred Fahrenheit, John and I set out for a walk to Tintinhull. We approached this favourite haunt of ours by way of Marsh Lane. At the entrance of Captain Chaffey's drive we stood talking to Denman. This old labourer had been a quarryman on Ham Hill for nearly eighty years. He had seen us from a distance, trailing along in white flannels through the Stoke Road dust. He accosted us. I began to think that the old man had already, early as it was, been drinking cider, for presently he laid his toil-encrusted hands upon us and cried out in a loud voice: 'Sixty years agone to-day come two months I was trapesing along this here turnpike road to ploughing match. Yes, we know as much of life as they that cross the ocean, we *that live on the deep soil*. We have *our* waves as well as the rest of them, we quarrymen, ploughmen, shepherdmen, come fine, come rain, come cold, come het.' The old chap was so filthy and made such a din as we stood there under the decorous copper beech, that I was glad to escape through the captain's white iron gates.

Presently we came by Wulham's Mill, that ancient mill which stands by its stream completely lost in meadows. We leaned over a gate. The grey roof, sunken with age, cut an uneven line against the sweltering sky. The place seemed held under a strange noonday glamour. There was never a rustle in the long potato-rows in the garden, not one small purple flower stirred. Except for a pregnant tabby-cat stretched out under a currant-bush at the edge of the stone-flagged path, there was no sign of life. It was here that the miller's little daughter had been drowned in the mill-pond, her body being seen by her father floating against the old, rusty, water-worn sluice. It was here, also, that I was to come two years later with Marion Linton.

At last we reached the churchyard, which we two had been in the habit of visiting for so many years. Not far from the old seventeenth-century altar-tomb of the family of Francis, we noticed a new grave, covered with Madonna lilies, such as were then in flower in all the cottage gardens. Whom had they buried here so recently, in this hot July weather? We moved across to the church porch, seeking shelter from the sun, and pushed open the heavy door which held in its oaken timber great nails deep embedded, nails driven home centuries before by the hands of dead Denmans, long since crumbled to dust, nails still able to respond, after the limited fashion of iron, to the divine sudorific influences of that unequalled day.

We had some bread and cheese at the Lamb. We gave a drink to a postman who came in. He said he preferred frosty weather. Not so an old tramp, who had once been a ship's steward. 'I likes this het,' he kept repeating, as large, silvery beads fell from his forehead. He had come from Yeovil, resting often, so he told us, in shady places. The ends of his boots had been slit to make them easier for walking. We bought a celluloid hair-comb from him for half a crown. The tavern parlour was cool as a well. A wasp was beating itself against a window-pane, and John must needs catch it in his handkerchief to let it out. How different was the smell of this interior from the smell of the church! And how the atmosphere of such a place lends itself to philosophic discourse! In a tavern one touches life at its centre. Here is the heart of the bee-hive. Here, at any rate, no spiritual treachery is tolerated; here, at any rate, no deceitful idealism stretches out tendrils white and sickly. . . . He who sits down on a tavern settle must even take the world as he finds it. He must know what birth means, and that we come into the world in no very cleanly manner; he must know what love means, and wrath, and lust, and, above all, death. In a tavern, come winter, come summer, the blunt truth will out. I had walked not long before to a village situated behind West Coker, and had observed the grave of a former clergyman of the place, with the words, 'A little while,' carved on the headstone. 'A little while!' 'A little while!' It would be known under the smoky rafters of the Lamb Inn that the Rev. Launders' body was to lie there in the churchyard for a great deal longer than 'a little while'. These pretty texts survive best in a confined and pretty atmosphere, but grow faint and frail in these snug hostels, where simple, honest men gather, men who are disposed to speak good words of the old bawdy earth, and who, like so many Grangousiers, delight to sit warming their ballocks before a fair fire. We paid our reckoning to Mrs. Mary Yard, our hostess, who looked very prim and dignified in her white cap, and stepped out into the giddy, merciless sunshine of the little front garden.

We now wandered into Tintinhull Great-Field. The grass was dry and slippery. We were making our way to Kiss-

Me-Down covert. On each side of us lay sultry orchards, with the trunks of ancient apple-trees, half fallen to the ground, like a host of tottering old men, which the sun had ensorcerised there. Lesser blues and gate-keepers flitted about our boots, the soles of which had been polished so smooth by walking over the fields. We found that the drove going up through Kiss-Me-Down was littered with straw. We trod silently. ''Tis as though the king of the owls were sick,' said John. Above Windmill we passed through a field of oats, the green stalks of which had already taken to themselves that amethystine tint characteristic of oat-straw when the grain is approaching maturity.

We were back in time for tea. In those days we were always wondering whether it was more pleasant to wash our hands before eating or to leave them still odorous of the countryside. Often, while we were still debating this nice point, we would hear the tea-bell ring, and without more ado would go downstairs, one behind the other, to find the rest of the family standing in their places, waiting for my father to say grace, before he began cutting up the two loaves of bread, which stood on their wooden platters before him, a brown loaf and a white cottage-loaf, the soft, crinkled crust of the latter being especially delectable when it came fresh from the ovens of the black-bearded baker.

When we had sat down, the old man, my father, rubbing his hands with delight at having his children around him, would ask us about our walk, and we would tell him that we had found the body of a dead heron down by Wulham's mill, and also a flower which we thought might be skullcap.

And at that he would send my sister Lucy to fetch his 'Bewick' and his 'Johns Botany' from his study. He would then read out extracts from the two volumes. And afterwards, with a look of boundless benevolence, he would rub his hands and say that he was glad that we boys had had an interesting walk. And at this my mother's face would become lit up with a smile, at once so radiant, so sweet, and so *ironic*, that I would forgive her for being in love with the side of the moon which turns itself away from the earth, and which has never once been seen by Tintinhull tipplers, as they stagger out of the public-house past the village stocks, past the great elm, and past the duck-pond. And she would lean over to John and stroke his hand; for she always loved him, her first-born, the best.

Meanwhile, Lord Eversley, who, as our father used to tell us, had taken the side of our great-grandmother Shaw in some peevish quarrel with the first Lord Lilford, would look down out of his gold frame with the set, supercilious stare of a man of the world. And presently we would ring for more butter, which would be brought in creamy and freshly churned, and then we would ring for more milk also, and have the white china jug with tomtits painted upon it refilled with what was all 'top of the pail'.

CHAPTER EIGHT

September

SOME TIME towards the end of that unequalled August, Bernard Price O'Neill came to Montacute. Perhaps, if I exclude my brother John, this incomparable Irishman has contributed more to my culture than anybody. How sensitive in his perceptions, how delicate in all his relationships, how unsurpassed as a companion! With a wit as light as a tomtit's feather, with a humour as sturdy and convoluted as the ear of a hedgehog, his presence bestowed a value, a significance, to every incident of the day. In that divine weather, to have his genius at my side was an unparalleled privilege. Together we walked along a thousand highways, along a thousand goosepaths, his round, well-favoured face gleaming under the broad brim of his panama hat as though it possessed a kind of lustre of its own, like the light in the tail of a glowworm.

There was no public-house within reach that we did not visit—The Choughs at Yeovil, The Carpenter's Arms at Chilthorne Domer, The Dolphin and The Hole in the Wall at Ilchester, The Half Moon and The White Horse at Martock, and the Portman Arms at Middle Chinock—our tongues, meanwhile, wagging in our heads as merrily as a pair of bell-clappers ringing in the new year. Often we would be content to sit by the side of a dusty road for hours together, chattering with glee like two chipmunks on a sunny wall. All was delectation, all was entrancement, our very excrement transformed. 'Ha! what divine mustard of the Gods!'

One morning, as we squatted on our haunches amongst some bracken, 'Cuckoo!' we called to a bullfrog who was regarding us from a mossy chink in a beech-tree bole. 'Cuckoo!' carolled the doctor. 'Perhaps,' said he, 'perhaps 'tis Diogenes!' And so wonderfully had the mood of my friend bewitched me, that I half came to believe that the soul of the old Greek was present with us in that spinney, through the wilting leaves of which the sempiternal sunshine sprinkled itself. We would be out of doors all day long. Before breakfast, even, we would wander down the village street, past Miss Sparks's shop, to sit, full of good talk, on the great stone coffin that had once contained an abbot's body, and which now lay under the south side of the church tower. Perhaps for the space of half an hour we would remain perched on the edge of that enormous sarcophagus, hollow as a nut, into the snug recess of which old George Wittle was to creep ten years later, drunk as a honey-fed bear, after Club-walking. The ringers found him in the evening, just as they were about to go up to the belfry. 'Well, I be damned!' one of them cried. 'If that bain't be wold George a-lying in wold coffin as snug as coney in burrow.' The befuddled labourer was immediately dragged out of his resting-place, still drowsy, but in a dim kind of way proud of his exploit. 'Well, George, thee knew well enough 'sknow not to be runned over by they motor-cars; the last trump be better, eh, George, though God A'mighty

He'd soon have gived 'ee gee up and no mistake if He'd a catched 'ee.'

Then we would leave the old stone coffin and wander over to my sister Nelly's grave, dead, poor lass, already eighteen years, and stand, for a moment, on the very spot of ground under which to-day lie the body of a man and the body of a woman, sleeping an unawakening sleep, untroubled by thoughts of turbulent children.

My brother Bertie, the architect, was at this time restoring Langport Church tower, and we went to visit him. He had a French governess to look after his daughter Isobel. And that night, as a red-glowing harvest-moon appeared over the horizon, projecting above the stubble like God's thumb, a troop of us frolicked and danced and sang in its sweet light. What laughter, what jollity! Over our heads the shrill bats flew, away in the lower meadows the corncrakes were calling, while near by, in the barley mow, the mice rustled, in that barley mow where I was happy, and whose every straw was daintily edged with silver. 'Tell me,' inquired the doctor, as he peered out of the dormer window, where we were sleeping, for a last look at the night, 'why is a young girl greater than the greatest philosopher?' I heard a cart-horse move in the barton over the way. I heard the distant barking of a farm-dog, and was silent. He had propounded a riddle that I could not answer.

The next day we returned to Montacute by way of Yeovil. We sat for an hour or two in the tap-room of The Choughs. The jackdaw face of Benjamin Disraeli looked down upon us from the wall opposite, as we drank by the stained wooden table, with the sound of the traffic of the market-town rattling past us outside. The sun slanted through the window upon the delf and the bottles behind the counter; and a little servant girl, who had been industriously sweeping out the inner parlour, passed by us, carrying in her hand a paper which contained the world's news for September 13, 1911. 'What a sweet-natured girl; fit to carry raspberries in her apron for Admiral Nelson!' observed Bernie, after she had shut the door.

We walked back by the sandy lanes. We came upon a blackbird lying dead in the dust. Its beak was as gold as a buttercup, and the feathers on its stiff body were as glossy-black as my father's cassock. We laid the bird in a sepulchre scooped out in the sandy wall of the lane. The Jews hid the body of Jesus in much the same way, long ago in Palestine. Alack! Between the body of a God and the body of a blackbird there is a wide difference, and what chance had these brittle bones of coming to life again, of extricating any more lubberly lobworms from their dew-moist tunnels?

I was sad when Bernie left to stay with my brother Willie in his dairy-farm at Witcombe. I heard from him the next day. 'Here sits Willie, my noble host, and cheek by jowl we write letters in the library of the farm on whose shelves many excellent books of the plough repose, and mark you, Bridlegoose, Lewes's History of Philosophy. Fancy the Joker who paid so much attention to Georgie Eliot being allowed to bear company with the sacred bull, the golden pigs, and the white cock of the Capitol, whom, however, not to put too fine a point on it, sacred or profane, Willie had slain for our dinner.'

One morning, while we were all seated round the Montacute breakfast-table, a robin hopped on to the stone sill of the French window and began eating the crumbs that my mother had put there, a merciful enough proceeding with the brown lawns as hard as though they were frozen. 'The robin,' announced my father, with solemn emphasis, 'is the only warbler that stays with us all the year round.' I had heard him impart this piece of information a hundred times. 'I hate robins, with their chirping domesticity,' remarked John in an undertone to me. As a matter of fact, the old man's interest in birds was always pretty to see. He cherished his schoolboy collection of eggs till he was in his eightieth year, preserving these little, brittle, multi-coloured shells till the day came when he had grown so simple that he could not for the life of him recall the name of a single one of them. At the latter end of his life I remember coming suddenly into his study one day, to find him sitting over them, touching them softly with his long fingers, troubled, perhaps, by some uncertain memory of the spring mornings when he had first taken them from their nests in Stalbridge Vale, where each one of them had been brought into the world by birds who, although in their day light of wing and full of song, were now lost beyond all record in an oblivion profound and absolute. He used to lead us out on bird-nesting walks when we were children, and give us instructions as to the taking of only one egg from a nest, lest the bird 'desert'. All the eggs we found he would blow for us, holding each fragile morsel of porcelain between his fingers, telling us, meanwhile, whether it was 'fresh' or 'hard-set'. Once, during those happy Easter holidays, when I used to go bird-nesting all day long with Bertie, scrambling through every hedge we saw, till our hands smelt of the young elder-twigs we had snapped, we found a hawfinch's nest. Now, this bird is extremely rare in the West of England, and we had never come upon its nest or seen its egg before. Wild with excitement, we rushed home. With such a trophy in our possession, we were no longer fearful of disturbing the old man in his study. His delight almost equalled ours. He compared it with the chaffinch's egg, with the greenfinch's egg, and, in the very middle of his morning's work, got out his 'Bewick'.

My father's 'study' had an interest of its own. A smell hung about it, such as one might imagine belonged to a bison, who, with clean hoofs and healthy hide, had just been driven in from some wild prairie. On the chimney-piece were set two silver cups, which he had won at Cambridge, the larger for boating, the smaller for a walking-wager. On the wall, to the left, hung his brother's sword, the sword of that same Uncle Littleton who had died in India of the cholera. Below the sword hung an extraordinary object, round and brown and heavy—an elephant's foot!— so we were told. In Africa, after I had been pursued by one of these animals, I remember recalling grimly enough that formidable piece of matter, which, because of its ill-defined shape, used so to puzzle me as a child.

'The study' represented my father's fort, his embattled sanctuary, from which, sustained by consultations with my mother, he was able to sally forth into the world with his personal dignity unchallenged, his personal pride unabated. How nervously would we children knock at the study door, either to consult him upon some matter of moment, or merely to ask for the use of the long stick of red sealing-wax which was always kept near his quill-pen. He liked to seal our packages for us. Very solemnly he would light one of the candles on his table and hold the scarlet stick in its flame, and from thence convey it, still burning, to the brown-paper parcel, upon which, in due time, when the wax had somewhat cooled, he would indent the Powys arms, from the gold seal on his watch-chain. And, this done, he would look up and smile with an expression of extra-ordinary benignity, like that on the face of a small boy who has carried through successfully some difficult undertaking. For his noble, leonine countenance could compose itself into very beneficent outlines, just as on occasions it could gather its contours into a composition sufficiently formida-ble to dominate the boldest of his headstrong children. And truly, how redoubtable the old man was capable of looking, with his low forehead, his long upper lip, and long tufted eyebrows! Even in the last years of his life, with his mind devoid of articulate thought, I have seen him stand at the window of his house at Weymouth and look out over the wide wintry spaces of the English Channel for hours together, with his grey eyes under his shaggy brows proud and undimmed as those of a king eagle. 'Looking out at what?' I used to wonder, as, glancing up from my book, I would be held spellbound by the terrific physiognomy belonging to an octogenarian who was reputed to be childish. The winds would howl and grey spray would rise from the waves, the sea-gulls would sweep over the deserted beaches, but the aged man, who still held himself erect in the cruel strait-jacket that the years had laid upon him, would look out beyond the wildly hovering sea-birds, beyond the tossing waves, beyond where the furthest horizon faded behind the dim promontory of St. Alban's Head.

On the afternoon of the same day that my father had commented upon the habits of the robin, I walked with him to Witcombe. He wished to speak with my brother Willie on some matter of business. By the Tintinhull turn, I think it was, or between that and the forge, he spoke of parish matters, and said that *he went on very quietly*. He said this with more pride than possibly can be conceived. All nature seemed to echo the words, as though celebrating the glory of God. 'He goes on very quietly,' said the ditch. 'He goes on very quietly,' cried the dung-hill. 'He goes on very quietly,' repeated a passing rook, flying in the direction of Kiss-Me-Down covert.

Witcombe was as pleasing to me as ever. It was merry to be walking again down the narrow, raised, stone causeway, brushed with long grasses from the hedge. In the small courtyard at the back of the house, the milk-pails were gleaming like the shields of heroes, while inside, the rooms were as cool as those of a moss-hut. The house was very old and very mellow, with sagging boards and dark beams, and a little peep-hole in the middle of the parlour door, through which I could see valerian growing on the front wall. I left my father talking to our nurse Emily, who, since he had taken the farm, had been Willie's housekeeper, and went off down the drove to the field near the river, where they were milking. Bernie was there. He had just picked up an emperor-moth caterpillar and was putting it into a cardboard box he had with him, and would keep it, he said, till it had spun 'its lovely flask-shaped cocoon in which to serenely await its resurrection'. We approached Willie, who was sitting on a three-legged stool, his head against Ruby's flank. We approached him circuitously, giving his Hereford bull, Dick, the widest possible berth. The churlish animal never took its eyes off us. When we were within safe running distance of Willie, Bernie stopped short, and, protruding his chin, contorted his round, gleaming features into a form which to him seemed to resemble that steady bovine stare. He remained motionless thus for several moments, with one foot planted in a cow-pat, and the other thrust slightly forward, in imitation of the bull.

Once at Willie's side, we were as jolly as two hedge-hogs who had come to suck at the udder of that wide-horned cow. And, indeed, old Will gave us some of its milk to drink, squirting it with much laughter straight out of a warm teat into our mouths.

At the end of the month, Bernie returned to London. He wrote to me: 'How are you, my dear young Prince?

September

What crystal thoughts are suspended in your brain, how moves the enchanting beauty of Montacute? Ralph told me you had a cold. I hope, therefore, by vigorous adherence to your wisely arranged manner of living, that you have expelled the little devil with his little red phyz and testy choler. Have you matured your plans for going to stay with Theodore? I hear he has killed his former philosophy and served it up on toast in a pretty, decorated dish of ascetic epicureanism. What delicious times we had! I hope you will like some olives I am sending you. Our Lord Montaigne must have rolled many under his tongue. I hear Hodder was happy with you. His head is like a coconut. Where is the gimlet that shall pierce its eye and let the milk flow out and the man spring forth? How sweet that milk was we drank in the fields!'

CHAPTER NINE

East Chaldon

NOW THAT the summer was over, it seemed wise to accept my brother Theodore's invitation to stay with him through the autumn. He lived then, as he still does, in the small village of East Chaldon, some two miles inland from those noble chalk headlands which rise one behind the other all along the sea-coast, from Weymouth to Lulworth Cove.

Never for a single moment, since he reached the age of discretion, has my brother Theodore given so much as a sunflower-seed for the busy practical life of our Western World, that shallow, unreflective life, which appears to be so exactly adapted to the taste of most Anglo-Saxons. He is like a sportsman who has left his fellow pheasant-shooters to go down into the marshlands after snipe. He is hunting a wild bird indeed, *a bird that flies zigzag*. He is hunting God.

At first, after disentangling himself from the practical occupation in which he was involved, he went to live at Studland, near Swanage. Presently, however, when even that picturesque place became overrun with summer tourists, he took his stick from his chimney-corner and set out to find some unpretentious village, where he would be altogether free from molestation. He walked on and on, over the downs. He went into Corfe, into Kimeridge, into Arishmell Bay, until eventually he arrived at Winfrith, and from there debouched to East Chaldon, which very possibly is the most hidden village in Dorset. And here, for twenty years, he has lived, occupied with his own queer mystical illuminations, with his books, his writing, and his wife and two boys. His house is surrounded by bare downs, over the huge, supine shoulders of which sea-gulls and black rooks alternately cast their shadows. There are foxes and rabbits on these exposed uplands, and now and again in one's walks one comes upon groups of stunted gorse bushes, which towards evening resemble flocks of gorgons, resting for a moment in a flight across the world, their talons clutching fast to the short turf which covers the flinty soil of those wind-swept hills. During the twenty years my brother has walked over those downs, never once, not for a day, has he forgotten his quest. With grey, haunted eyes he has scanned the denuded, immemorial outlines of the hills. With ears pricked up like a cat's in a kitchen, he has listened to the village priest and the village pauper. Like a melancholy-eyed beagle moving in and out of the bracken, he has smelt God and will not be called off. For more than a quarter of a century he has been the manœuvring, incorrigible eavesdropper, who is always on the alert to hear, through cranny or keyhole, what God says *when He talks to Himself*.

I left Montacute on October 25th, and found Theodore waiting for me on the platform of my dear natal town of Dorchester. He had allowed his beard to grow, and he looked like some moujik strayed into Wessex, as different from the burghers of the old Roman town as a racoon in a settlement of woodchuck.

That afternoon we walked together to Ringstead Bay, a low valley which lies directly to the right of where the Great White Nore projects its proud promontories into the Channel, those same proud, immaculate promontories that I was to observe, years afterwards, gradually taking form out of the mists of the horizon, as I sailed up the English Channel, standing alone at the prow of a great liner, my eyes blind with tears, home at last after my exile in Africa. I was in high spirits to be near the sea again, and felt, as I inhaled the salt air of those lone beaches, that my cough, which had again been causing me anxiety, could not fail now to get better. With the ancestral quiver passing through me, I ran down over the sounding shingle to dip my hands in the sea!

Coming back across the downs, we stood for a moment to watch the sun sink. Behind Abbotsbury, behind the Chesil beach, the Atlantic rose like a long, low, slate-coloured wall. It was as though we two were looking at the last rampart of the world.

To wake each morning in my small room, with the clearer, lighter air of Dorset all about me, was wonderful. It was an air that had to do with high, drifting, fine-weather clouds, so different from the air of Somerset, which always seemed during the autumn months to carry with it the breath of Witcombe Bottoms or of the withy-bed near Bride's Mead, or exhalations from those toadstools of faery colours, at that time of the year to be seen in every copse and spinney. From my bed, as I lay that first morning, I could make out the forms of two men hurdling sheep on the hills opposite, and the sound of the animals they were tending came to my ears mingled with the sounds that Theodore was making downstairs, as he broke dry sticks over his knee before the fire.

My sister Philippa also stayed with Theodore during this autumn, and many were the happy walks I took with that mysterious and singular girl, who herself would sometimes appear to be the embodiment of the wind she so much loved. On many a rough November afternoon we descended the narrow, winding path which trailed past her beloved elder bush down to the very foot of the White Nore. Often twilight would have fallen before we reached the water.

Never before had I spent an autumn by the sea, and I was excited by these long, deserted, desolate winter beaches. How the waves beat against the chalk rocks, and advanced, and receded, and advanced again over those cold banks of shining pebbles! As always when in close contact with Nature, Philippa became transfigured. 'I am the hills!' she cried. 'The sea is my lover. . . . Yes, I am at ease and understood on these downlands. Once upon them, and all is forgotten.' As we came up her favourite gully, I was almost alarmed, as I looked at her small head, crooning and muttering to the wind. What passionate and intractable spirit had not God imprisoned in my sister's body!

Sometimes, of an early Sunday morning, I would enter the old grey church to take the sacrament. The crisp air outside, each straw on the road having hoar-frost upon it, made a brave contrast to the stuffy, half-darkened interior of the building, where, before a primitive altar, a bereft priest would raise a chalice aloft in a devout ecstasy. And as I knelt with bowed head to partake of the beautiful, antique ritual, I would try to conceive what inner secret the wild rumour held, so that it could survive generation after generation, wherever two or three might be gathered together. And with the curious peace of the place all about me, with the cold bare trees in the churchyard hedge visible through the leaded window-panes, with the candle-lighted chancel, and with the Vicarage man-servant and maid-servant in the pew at my side, I would feel half inclined to believe also. Why not? Why should not I, also, become as a little child and go to Heaven along with the Master of Corpus?

Then a different mood would come upon me. I would hear a strutting rooster in Farmer Tod's farmyard call reveille to his sely pullets, and immediately I would begin wondering what in the devil's name could have started the 'crazy story, going so crazy, crazy'. And like a green-crested poll-parrot, whose foolish head can think only of peeled almonds, I would nod and nod again at that homely altar, with its tall, spluttering, yellow candles.

In the afternoon I would perhaps walk over the downs with Theodore to the stone circle above Poxwell—or Puck's Well, as it was originally called—that stone circle put into place by other priests, centuries before any such extraordinary notion had come into God's head as to send down to earth His only-begotten son to be sacrificed by

Himself, to Himself. One day Theodore commented upon the grass of his chosen habitation. 'I like this long, white, downland grass,' he said. 'Nothing ever eats it, and it's like the curious grey hairs of some old woman. It never gets wet. In summer I often roll in it.' That afternoon we came back by the sea, and Theodore selected from the beach a round, white pebble. 'To use,' he said, 'when I darn my stockings.'

CHAPTER TEN

Seaside Air

I USED TO like to wake, each morning, to see the wintry sunshine upon the short turf of the frosted downs. I would hear Theodore moving about below. 'Go out, you cats,' he would say; and a few minutes later the crackling of a fire in the parlour would become audible. I would then hurriedly dress, lest I should be too late to go with him to the village to fetch the milk. How happy we would be during those short excursions before breakfast! How we would tiptoe past the gate of the sombre Victorian vicarage, past the churchyard, and down over the crisp, stiff grass of the village green!

One morning, on our way back, we saw the sun like an All Hallow-e'en pumpkin framed under the belly of one of Farmer Tod's carthorses, the illuminated hairs of the animal's rough winter coat appearing like a sacred nimbus. And what divine chat we would have as we sat with hooked knees and lighted cigarettes over our last cup of tea!

It was on just such a morning that we set out across Egdon Heath to visit a tavern called The Seven Sisters, on the other side of Giddy Green. The sun caressed the heath, and the moorland streams flowed merrily along in their black peat beds, each piece of gravel below their crinkled waters shining like a tiny nugget of gold. Theodore looked about him, an expression of miching mallecho flickering across his goblin features. I could not tell what was amusing him; but soon he said, 'You don't find the aspect of the moor, on such a day as this, described by Thomas Hardy.' However, the day was not destined to remain fine; for presently the wind backed to the south, and the sky became overcast. We rested on the side of a tumulus, which lay like an enormous, inverted urn in the centre of the brown waste. To the right, at the top of a sandy pit, stood a single fir tree, stunted, storm-riven. We noted how the ground below the heather was covered with an exquisite web of white lichen. Presently from the direction of the fir tree, came a rabbit, with a stoat after it. It was overtaken in the gravel-pit below. We heard its cries, as, rolling over and over, it felt the teeth of its vicious enemy sink into its jugular vein. Theodore ran forward and began throwing stones into the brambles, wherever he judged the struggling rabbit was. I stood by his side, feeling, I am ashamed to say, a kind of exultation in the thought of what was taking place. It gave me, I confess it, a sharp, attenuated refreshment to think of the tussle, down there below, between the mild-eyed, harmless, soft-furred creature and its lithe enemy, muscular and merciless.

On more than one occasion in my life I have been startled by discovering the presence in me of such lively emotions. One day, from the door of my hut in Africa, I shot at a white-breasted hawk. The bird fell from the bough of the dead olive tree upon which it had settled. My kitchen *mtoto*, a Kikuyu boy, of about fourteen years, having observed what had happened, came round from the outhouse to ask

me if he could have it. Knowing how the natives delight
in decorating their heads with white feathers, I told him to
go and pick it up. Ten minutes later, happening to come
out of my house for something, I found the boy and a little
naked girl lolling on either side of the unfortunate bird,
which they had spreadeagled on the ground with pegs. It
was still alive, and these two children of Africa were occupied in slowly and deliberately torturing it to death. Now
you would have thought that an English gentleman, brought
up at an English public school and at an English university,
a man who had been so sensitive as a child that he could
not bear to see a horse struggling up Hollow Lane with a
load of Ham Hill stones, or even a mouse drowning desper-
ately in a bucket of water, would have felt outraged to the
centre of his being by what those two children were doing.
Not at all. In a flash it was revealed to me then how powerful
a current in life is this particular blood-hot emotion. For
no sooner had I realised what it was that was causing those
delicate ebon lips to curl in so lovely, in so excited a
manner, than I felt myself caught up in a gust of passion
that went quivering through my frame like wind through
a quaking asp, a gust of passion that remained shameless
and conspiring, and which gave its complete sanction to
what was taking place. Indeed, it was only by the greatest
effort of will that I stepped forward to put the proud white-
breasted hawk out of its misery; and I daresay, as a matter
of fact, I would not have interfered at all, had I not known
that my brother Willie might appear at any moment.

Theodore and I walked now in the direction of Bindon

Abbey, the same ruined Abbey into the hallowed precincts of which Angel Clare carried Tess on the night after their wedding. Here, truly, was melancholy. Before ever we had reached the ruins, it had begun to rain. They were surrounded by a moat of clear water, the bottom of which was parqueted with spotted sycamore leaves. Rain drifted through the stripped trees above our heads, and in large drops pattered down upon our drenched and sopping greatcoats. I crossed over to the place where the high altar had once stood, and thought of the masses that had been celebrated there at Christmas, at the Feast of St. John, at the Feast of St. Stephen! The nostrils of how many dead monks, buried under my feet, had inhaled the same autumnal smells that even now rose from the garth. Coming back behind Winfrith, we passed through a field of swedes. 'Nothing in Nature,' said Theodore, 'suggests freshness and purity as much as do swedes against the brown mould, their smooth shining leaves blown by the wind, and each root so snug in the ground.'

It was during that November that I received a letter from Wilbraham, telling me that he was ill and had taken refuge in a sanatorium at Bournemouth. I went to visit him. I reached the old seaport of Poole before ten o'clock in the morning. With delight I walked along the quayside. I came to a grass-grown square, over against the water, shut in on two sides by sober red-brick lodging-houses, and here I curled up under some fishing nets to eat an apple I had bought for a penny, and to read John's letter. 'I whirl about from Ohio to Michigan, and from Michigan to Missouri,

and as I travel to and fro I sometimes experience fear, fear
of trains, of crowds, of hotels, of all the outward, of all
that "sticking out" aspect of things which looks so sarcastic
upon us poor sensitive decadents. A mad, exposed, morbid
person in America, that would be a bitter subject for a
book. I act my rôle well enough; but oh, how tired I am
of lecturing! When you have got to the top of anything,
you always find nothing. I must, my darling, tell you how
I have loved your letters all this while, so regularly sent. I
have been transported into precisely that leisurely world
you speak of, of trailing bootlaces, and half-lit cigarettes,
and hesitant departures over dewy fields, and low-breathed
dramatic conspiracies, while below the voice we know
ascendeth unto the throne. I have been reading a new life
of Voltaire. There was a man indeed! Twice an intimate
friend of his carried off his girl and had her; but Voltaire
did not allow such incidents to disturb the harmony of the
situation. Like Lulu, he would say, "What has happened?
Nothing makes any difference. You are you, and I am I,
and our darling Pimpette is as she was! Why then a lot of
fuss?" So all three played and sauntered through the boulevards. And Voltaire records it afterwards in this lovely
manner: "Que nous nous aimions tous trois. Que nous
étions heureux!" '

I took a tram-car to Bournemouth and with no great
difficulty found the sanatorium. I was shown into Wilbraham's room and sat by an open window looking out on a
lawn, where two or three revolving shelters stood. I think
consumptive hospitals are even more depressing in the damp

of England than in the cold of Switzerland. The look of
bedclothes, the look of white sheets against the chilled,
green grass of an English tennis-lawn in winter, could anything possibly be more devastating? Wilbraham gave me a
volume of Yeats's poems. His temperature was high, and
he had the fluttered, preoccupied look of a man who knows
that he is dying. Towards evening I escaped from the devilish
place, and, hurrying through the smug, modern streets of
Bournemouth, came down to the sea. I walked along the
deserted sands towards Boscombe pier. To be alive, only
to be alive, may I never forget the privilege of that! The
setting sun had left a yellow glow in the sky, which was
reflected upon the water. Small waves kept lap-lapping over
the crisp flats, across which I walked, brisk and jocund,
testing with sensitive weasand the particular quality of the
frosty seaside air.

CHAPTER ELEVEN

A Smuggler's Path

I SPENT MANY hours during that autumn scrambling about the chalk cliffs to the left of the White Nore. From an old fisherman I learnt the names of each headland, West Bottom, Middle Bottom, Bat's Head, Scratchy, Swyre Head, Big Durdle, Mupe Rocks, Cock Pit, Arishmell. Below Middle Bottom there stretches a beach, about a mile in length, shaped like a crescent moon, and impossible to be reached except by boat. I would often stand with Theodore and peer down upon that curved bank of shelving shingle, cleansed and cleansed again by wind and waves and rain. From where we used to stand we could hardly hear the waves breaking, so far below us were they, and so wildly did the sea-gulls scream, as they swept backwards and forwards, with open beaks, over that blue abyss.

One morning, as I walked along Middle Bottom, I noticed a rabbit disappear over the cliff's edge. On coming to the place, I made out a kind of ledge, down which a man might possibly clamber to a rocky projection, some forty feet below. Immediately I was seized with a great desire to reach this point. The fisherman had told me that smugglers in the old days had frequented this bay, and it seemed to me that I had probably found the top of the path used by them when scaling the cliff. Very slowly, scarcely venturing to look at the wrinkled sea below me, I clambered down, foot by foot. Once on the other side of the rock, I came upon a rusty iron bar, deeply embedded in the face of the bluff. I reached it, and held to it with both hands, as the only stable thing on the side of that tilted precipice. My knees trembled. The idea of climbing back terrified me, the idea of climbing down terrified me. And yet, how exciting, if only I could manage to reach that purged and chastened beach, at which I had so often gazed! Again I descended. There was a kind of track. Once I dislodged a small stone and shivered to see how it fell with scarcely a break to the pebbles so far below.

I was a full hour in the solitary cove. I trudged from one end to the other of its virginal beach, shaped like a horned moon. I came upon a dead sea-gull and cut off its wing to carry back as a gift to my sweet sea-gull sister. Under Bat's Head I found a cave, and crawled into its further recesses where I lay for a time listening to the boom-boom of the waves, as they rolled in upon the hollow tunnels, honey-combing that solitary headland. The cave was full of sea-weed, and I picked up a long brown riband and bound it round my forehead. Its surface was smooth and slippery, and no mermaid could have smelt more intimately of the sea.

Walking back to the place where I would have to begin the ascent, I looked up. All was blue and white—white cliffs and blue sky, white surf and blue sea, white birds and blue, curling waves! I felt giddy. I could see the smuggler's stake sticking out of the precipice like a nail in a white-washed wall. When I had scaled some fifty feet, I looked round. There below me were the tracks I had made in the wet, red shingle. Above, the cliff flanked itself against the sky like a snow-covered alp. I began climbing again, and in a few minutes was once more clinging to the corroded iron stake. Only faintly now there came to my ears the monotonous ebb and flow of the sea, insistent and resonant as the respiration of some sleeping Cerne Giant.

On the way back over the downs, it began to rain, and I spent the afternoon lying on the sofa by the window. Before I lit my lamp, my eye fell with a heightened sense of consciousness upon the window-panes, splashed and bespattered with raindrops. Perhaps I could have looked wittingly upon no material objects better able to make me aware of my existence than those flat rain-washed sheets of glass, which appeared to me then so colourless and melancholy, so suggestive, in the fading light, of every wet afternoon that I had ever known. Theodore came in, and I realised at once that he was sunk in one of his worst moods of depression. His features had the same dreary look that was presented by the patient window-panes with the grey rain trickling down them. We talked together. 'In this life, all we can do,' he said, 'is each day so to tire our limbs that rest is acceptable—and finally death.' I spoke of the blessedness of life, but he would have none of it. 'For a pint of honey a gallon of gall, for a dram of pleasure a pound of pain, for an inch of mirth an ell of moan. For as ivy doth encompass the oak, so do our miseries encompass our lives. Your philosophy is false,' he cried, with more emotion than I had ever known him to display, 'false, false, and again false.

We must learn to welcome Death. Death is the great Father of all things; for without him there is no Life.'

Certainly Theodore is capable of becoming more hopelessly unhappy than any of us; and on such occasions his finely moulded face, with *its* long upper lip, takes upon it an expression of such utter dejection, that one can only catch one's breath, as if one had passed the Iscariot, rope in hand, walking towards his elder tree, that same elder tree whose aromatic, pith-filled twigs were still quick when Sir John Mandeville visited Palestine seven hundred years ago. But then, again, when he has not seen too much of you, when he thinks he has enough money in his tea-chest to store his cellar with coal, when he thinks the common people regard him with a friendly eye, when he thinks his mattresses do not smell of old bones, as John once had the temerity to suggest, and when he knows that you are not making love to any *very young* girls, then he will have his days, his hours, his moments. On such occasions the most unexpected observations will come from his mouth, one after the other, like sparks from a Twelfth-Night bonfire; his sardonic, dry quips, his double-tongued chirpings, jumping this way and that like crickets in a hot hay-field.

Bertie turned up one afternoon. He had come down to see some building in the neighbourhood, and had brought with him another architect. We all went a walk together. The conversation turned on 'The Society for the Preservation of Ancient Buildings', of which my brother Bertie has been for many years the secretary. 'This devotion,' said Theodore, 'for old things, old houses, old furniture, is often exaggerated out of all due proportion. Why, a human child is older than all these.' There has always been a certain inclination on Theodore's part to make sport of this particular brother, who, not even excepting Littleton, has done more 'honest work' in his life than all the rest of us put together. Perhaps Theodore is provoked by his direct, downright, positive manner, he himself being ever indirect in his advances and retreats, ever addicted to perfidious prevarications and ironic acquiescences. It was dark before we reached the quarry, but, as we came over the Five Marys, at the point of the road where the old thorn bush is which has been bent like a well-used besom by a thousand gales from the south-west, the moon suddenly swung into view, like an enormous lantern, on the left of Flower's Barrow.

We had seen two things of interest in our walk, a few sprays of winter jasmine nodding under the shelter of a West Chaldon cottage, and some farm-boys, with holly in their caps, showing their feeling that Christmas was not far off. When Theodore was taking off his gaiters by the fire, and I was unlacing my boots, there was the sound of laughter and quick movement across the floor upstairs. 'What are they making all that noise about up there?' asked Theodore, with simulated peevishness. 'You never know what they will be up to next, these architects, when they get together.' A few days after Bertie's departure, this letter arrived for Theodore: 'How are your funds? Could you put me up for the New Year, for booze-night; could you or

Lulu provide drink?' It was answered after the following manner: 'If you come on booze-night, to-day three weeks, you will have to pay ten shillings. We all pay our share. If you come any other night, no drink at all.

> *See and Hear*
> *Wine is dear.'*

When Theodore's birthday came, five days before Christmas, I gave him a fine blizzard-lantern, which I had bought in Dorchester, for him to use when he went out to his shed at night to chop up sticks.

CHAPTER TWELVE

A Christmas Eve

IT LOOKED as if we were going to have a green Christmas. For days on end it continued to rain so that presently we could hardly conceive the smoke from the chimneys blowing from any other direction than the south-west. Theodore and I planned to do our shopping on Christmas Eve. On December twenty-fourth, therefore, we had an early breakfast and set off over the moor to catch the train into Dorchester. It was not raining when we started, though the sky was heavy with clouds. As we were shutting the white gate out of the garden, the postman arrived and handed me a letter from Switzerland. I opened it, to find that Wilbraham, who in desperation had fled back to Davos Platz, was dead.

As we passed the Vicarage gate, I noticed how out at the elbow, out at the knee, out at the heel, Theodore was. In those days I had not yet learnt how little it matters whether a man has a good cloak over him or not. From my childhood I had always entertained certain middle-class prejudices, and I was still too close to Sherborne and Cambridge not to set considerable store by a new pair of breeches. He took my protest in good part; but even as I was speaking, I felt ashamed; aware as I was, that however ragged his jacket might be, he himself remained inflexibly loyal to a certain poetic conception of the world which in its intoler-

ance of the vulgar and the commonplace set him once and
for all outside ordinary standards.

When the train drew up at Morton, we got into a carriage with some country people, who were also going into
town to do their shopping. Theodore remarked how one
of the children, a little girl of fourteen years, was still
wearing her summer hat, a shady straw hat, which looked
pathetic enough when we got out at the South Western
Station to find that it had again begun to rain. Presently
we were walking along one of those stately avenues, the
trees of which were planted by French prisoners at the
time of the Napoleonic wars. Over the high wall which
surrounds its gardens I saw the solidly built Victorian
chimneys of the house in which I was born. How often
have I not tried to reconstruct for myself that occasion
when opportunity was given for me to be created! By what
auspicious hazard was a way prepared, during the autumn
of the year of our Lord 1883, for me to appear on this
round world, the eighth child of Charles Francis and Mary
Cowper, a unique composite of the dust of a million pro-
genitors, allowed, in its turn, an ephemeral existence, in
which to see, to smell, to hear, to taste, and to touch?
Surely the brave nature of the reversion granted to me on
that far-off night cannot be gainsaid. Let these devilish,
badger-headed scientists reduce all matter to a series of
revolving electrons, it still remains a sublime miracle of
miracles that man, with brittle egg-shell skull, should have
raised himself out of the dust. To open delicately contrived
eyelids on this earth, on this fifth-smallest of the planets,

which like a flock of frightened birds keep sailing about the sun, is surely a chance beyond all chances. It would be better to be a midget than a dead stone, it would be better to be a mud-eating lobworm under the ground than a dead stone, better to be a white-bellied beetle in Pitt Pond than a dead stone, and better, how much better, to be a cogitating mammal, firmly set upon his heels, capable of prevision, capable of retrospection, capable of wittolry.

And the fact that I was eventually born in the month of August, 'born in a corn-field', as John declares, has always been a satisfaction to me. Down in the West of England those four weeks have a character of their own. They know nothing of the mystical intimations which belong to the spring, and yet, at the same time, they are void of the sombre tints of cold annihilation that one comes to associate with the fall of the year. This month of Cæsar Augustus is a hot, good-natured, casual month. During its thirty-one days the foison of many a broad acre grows ready for the harvest; indeed, the countryside, far and near, lies basking under its hedges, like some swart, amorous dairy-wench, in sultry contentment, her vagrant longings at last completely satisfied. In the month of August the power of the Priest is at its nadir. Let him raise pale, vestmented hands before never so many ornate altars, let him thunder in the garb of an evil crow from never so many Puritan pulpits, it will profit him little. Behold! the grain grows golden in its husk, the green apples swell on their whorled twigs, and the shell of each hazelnut is neatly fitted with its ivory kernel. What have we to fear?

It was growing dark before we were ready to leave the gay, lighted streets, which, in spite of the heavy downpour, were so filled with festive faces. Theodore had bought a sledge-hammer for breaking up his coal, and with this primitive implement over his shoulder we began our walk, the rain blowing in gusts against our muffled figures, the naked hedgerows on each side of the old Wareham highway only dimly visible. A glimmer of light shone through the trees surrounding Max Gate. We thought of the old man in there, sitting by his apple-wood fire, brooding on God knows how many past Christmas nights; the old man whose genius we so loved and honoured. On we went, the sentinel elms by the field-gates appearing and disappearing. Now and then a tranter's van would overtake us, its dim, swaying lantern throwing upon our drenched forms a momentary illumination. As we came up over Broadmayne hill we remembered that we knew the clergyman of the place, an eccentric, bigoted, old-fashioned Calvinist, who lived with his two daughters, whose wits, together with those of their father, had been well-nigh turned by so much reading of the Bible. We determined to call at his house. It stood a little way back from the village street, a dark, gloomy vicarage, with the plaster falling from its walls. We turned towards it. On that Christmas Eve it presented to us a perfectly negative front. No light shone from any of its windows, from any of those tall, black, upstair windows, those heavy sashes were surely never opened to let fresh air into the bare, loveless bed-chambers they sheltered! We pulled at the bell. A hollow clack-clack-clack sounded, like the falling of a tin plate on a scullery floor. We waited. We could hear singing in the village; but except for this, and the sound made by a broken gutter emptying its water into the blackness of some shrubs to our left, there was nothing to disturb the forlorn quietude of the place.

We turned to go, and then, from somewhere, from some room far removed from the lidless windows at which we gazed, we heard the unmistakable sound of a door opening. A moment later and one of the girls was at the threshold, holding in her hand a guttering candle, the light of which made visible each raindrop falling at that particular moment between our eyes and her small, soberly dressed figure. We were conducted into the kitchen at the back of the house. The old man was out, they told us. He had gone to the bedside of a dying woman. The two girls made us welcome. They put a heavy iron kettle on to a fire, made in a grate which still held the grey ashes of many previous fires. I don't think I ever enjoyed a supper more than this one with these two extraordinary girls, whose minds had been given so odd a twist by the theological whimsies of their father, and whose demure bodies were so obviously never destined to be held in the free, unscrupulous arms of a lover. Our sudden appearance, out of the dark night, evidently excited them, and they set before us a fine feast, with toast, and bread-and-butter, and goose-eggs, and 'braun of tuskéd swyne'. With shining eyes, and quaint mouths awry with merriment, they listened to the stories of our day's adventures, their work-boxes and the garments they were making for the poor of the parish put away for once, on the side of the dresser. With a look of infinite deference on his astounding pigwiggen features, Theodore listened to everything either of them said; indeed, with his sledge-hammer leaning against his chair, he addressed them as if they had been princesses in disguise.

Before we left, the elder of the two put a large black-covered Bible before him, requesting that a chapter should be read. And so it came to pass that I found myself on this anniversary of Our Lord's birth listening to my brother's well-modulated voice intoning the sacred Scriptures. He selected to read from the sixth chapter of the Book of the Prophet Amos; and it seems to me that I can still hear the voice of this atheist, who is by his nature so profoundly religious, 'reading a chapter' over that kitchen table. We all four of us knelt on the uncarpeted floor. I watched a small mouse that kept running out from behind a basket of sticks. Once my eye rested on the figure of Joan, who knelt before me in rudely cobbled boots, with clasped hands raised above her head. And I suppose, until I am dead, the august, admonitory words that came to my ears will be associated with a little, frolicsome Christmas mouse, with a bespattered window as seen under a coarse calico blind, with the ecstatic look on a praying woman's face. 'Woe to them that are at ease in Zion . . . that lie upon beds of ivory, and stretch themselves upon their couches, and eat the lambs out of the flock and the calves out of the midst of the stall; that chant to the sound of the viol, and invent to themselves instruments of music, like David; that drink wine in bowls, and anoint themselves with the chief ointments . . . which rejoice in a thing of nought, which say, Have we not taken to ourselves horns by our own strength?'

CHAPTER THIRTEEN

A New Year's Eve

ON NEW Year's Eve my brother Littleton came to visit us. Nobody had concerned himself more about my illness than he. It was through his exertions that I originally went to Switzerland and he was now anxious to persuade me to return there for a few months, so as to avoid the treacherous English spring. I saw him off at Wool, and he got into a carriage with the Rev. Hugh Upton. I had not seen the Rev. Hugh since I had left school. The aura of his personality seemed to have pervaded every crevice of the dusty, upholstered, first-class carriage in which he sat. There had been always something unctuous and self-satisfied about him. I had remarked this fact even as a boy, when I had watched him one summer afternoon crossing the school-field, adorned in a Trinity Hall black-and-white cricket blazer. What a supercilious soul his smile betrayed, and how incredibly complacent the man looked now, with his legs wrapped round with an expensive travelling rug! The schoolmasters of English public schools, what a set they are! How limited! How provincial! Well I know them with their shallow routine minds. Well I know them with their fussy preoccupation over the sexual chastity of their charges, content if they can turn out into the world, year by year, young men, devoid of imagination, devoid of any social conscience outside their own class, and completely incapable of philosophic thinking; young men, whose sole accomplishment would seem to be in a state of Holy Matrimony, to propagate others like unto themselves. The mere thought, as I sit here in Montoma, with a score of blue-jays rattling in the Indian corn outside, in the corn which should have been harvested long ago and is now frosted and dry, the mere thought of these schoolmasters puts me out of humour.

It is wonderful how wisely emancipated Littleton has remained, seeing that he has lived at close quarters with them for so many years. Even at its height, his passion for athletics was never able to dull for him the pleasure he derived from nature and literature. Some of the happiest hours of my life have been spent at his side, walking over the turf of Corton Downs, thyme-scented and pliant underfoot, walking from Montacute to Pilsdon, to get our first glimpse of the sea, the blue, straight line of it suggesting to us, fresh from our inland orchards, so large a liberation; walking up through Porlock, up through the Horner woods, to the wild moors around Dunkery Beacon, where the smell of burnt heather would rise from the ground, and the cry of curlews be upon the wind. As a small boy, how thrilled I used to be by his athletic prowess, how thrilled to come on to the school-ground and see his familiar and beloved figure at the wicket, so strong, so lithe, so light of action! In the old days at Montacute, he used to play cricket for the village. I can now hear the back gate slam to on a summer evening, revealing him in the yard, with his long-shaped cricket-bag in his hand. And how, upon such occasions, I would leave my play and run to him, and ask him 'how many he had made', and follow him upstairs to his room, to the West Room, and stay talking with him until he was ready to come down to the dining-room, where my mother would be waiting for him with his supper on the table. And then, when he was seated at his place, at the right of my father's chair, my mother would go to him and kiss that clear forehead, free from all guile, and listen, working at her sewing, to all that he would relate, as he ate his cold mutton, his lettuce, and his stewed rhubarb, about the soft rose-pink stalks of which the milk from the tomtit jug would curdle.

At supper that night, Theodore and I decided that we would walk over the downs to the Stone Circle. We had a fancy to see the old year out within the circumference of that heathen cromlech. It was a frosty night. As soon as the white garden-gate had clicked back on to its latch, we found that the road under our feet was no longer muddy, but was already sparkling in the starshine. Away we went, past the old barn, past the field where the sea-gulls collect, our walking-sticks hitting on the resonant ground, and one topic of conversation following on the heels of another, like baboons along an escarpment ledge. As we came through the farmyard at West Chaldon, we paused to watch a labourer, in the long, thatched stable giving fodder to his horses. The look of that warm interior, in this last day of the year, hay-smelling, harness-smelling, horse-smelling, put us in mind of the simple lives of these people, and of how the seasons pass over their heads in swift succession, from sowing-time even unto ploughing-time, and how they take it all as calmly and naturally as the old draught-mare we could even now see, with outstretched neck and thick prehensile lip, nuzzling at the hay in the rack above its head.

Once on the downs, all was clear and translucent. Fold upon fold of these ancient hills lay before us in all their midnight beauty. We would come to a gate with the rime gleaming upon its top bar, open it, and pass on to an upland, even more remote, more secluded. We passed the grey wall, near where, in the early autumn, we had one day filled our handkerchiefs with button-mushrooms, cold mushrooms so sweet that even in their raw state it was pleasant to nibble at them. We passed the holly-hedge from which we had gathered red berries to decorate our room for Christmas, the very places where we had broken off branches clearly visible in the starlight.

At last we were there. Theodore entered the ring first, the shadow of his bowed figure—he had taken his old cloak about him—appearing, as it fell across the deep-sunken stones, like the shadow of some Biblical prophet, like the shadow of the prophet Amos! And with what curious, prophetic eyes he squinnied up at the sky during those still, frosty moments!

We were silent. There we stood, in the enchanted circle, like two fools, like two conjured haggards, looking out beyond the great square of Pegasus, beyond the Milky Way, to the furthest, uncharted tracts of a material Universe without beginning and without end.

CHAPTER FOURTEEN

'Timor Mortis Conturbat Me'

I PERSUADED THEODORE to leave his retreat for once and travel with me as far as Folkestone. He wrote to some friends of his at Aldeburgh, asking whether he could stay with them for three days on his way back. He penned the note in his meticulous handwriting, every single letter being formed with exaggerated care, as though they were hieroglyphics. 'Surely,' he said, when at last he had finished, 'surely they can put up with me for three days. Why the Jews put up with Jesus for thirty years.' How individual he looked, as he stood on the quay, waving his stick! The well-dressed people by whom he was surrounded appeared like so many ninnies in contrast with this bearded man, in dark clothes, who hunts for God as a collector hunts for a great auk's egg. And what a knowing, sidelong, twisted glance he had given me, as the train slid past the great Necropolis at Woking!

I had arranged to go to Arosa, a small winter-resort in the Engadine as far as I knew unvisited by consumptives. One reached there by Coire, driving from there some twenty miles by sleigh. I had selected to stay in the best hotel of the place. Its door was opened to me by an enormous, gold-braided porter, and a moment later I found myself in a lighted hall resounding with high-pitched, English voices. If I were to see the same people to-day, I daresay I should think very little of them. As it was, I felt impressed. Their assurance, their correct dress, their constant use of 'sporting slang', intimidated me. I did not realise, as I came to realise later, that these people were regarded with nothing but amused contempt by the real aristocracy, who, demanding above everything else individuality, would not give a purple mulberry for an assemblage of this kind, where everybody was trying to behave exactly like everybody else. What added to my own immediate discomfiture, however, was the discovery, when I came down to dinner the first evening, that all the men were wearing dinner-jackets instead of tail-coats. I felt indignant that Littleton, who, as a general rule is up to the mark in such matters, had not thought of telling me the correct fashion in dress for hotel dining-rooms. To have to enter, each night, the resplendent *salle-à-manger*, and walk across to my table in my tail-coat, was to me an extremely humiliating ordeal. I came to dread the evenings, came to dread the time when it was necessary for me to sally out of my bedroom, and would feel no sense of ease until I had reached my chair and had the offending appendages safely concealed under me. And even then, I had only to rise to leave the room, and I would feel as if the eye of every waiter and every guest were riveted on the superfluous part of my dress. So great was my mortification that I was rendered incapable of regarding the situation humorously. In truth, one downward glance of the sardonically obsequious, gold-braided porter, as I reached the foot of the wide, carpeted stairs, would be sufficient to disrupt any state of philo-

sophic composure which I might have attained in the
solitude of my chamber. Even after I had made friends with
the few distinguished people who were staying in the hotel,
and had thereby cunningly formed a screen between myself
and the rest, who now no longer dared to look at me askance,
I still experienced moments of extreme self-consciousness;
as when two young popinjays, finding me settled in a
favourite corner of theirs, warmed by a radiator, expressed
their annoyance by the use of the two words, 'hard cheese',
a phrase which, though doubtless natural enough to them,
seemed to me, so hypersensitive had I become, to suggest a
kind of sneering contempt for my presence, a contempt I
could only attribute to the fact that I must appear to them
utterly absurd, sitting there with my coat-tails tucked so
carefully out of sight.

Soon after I arrived, I took my temperature, and found
that it was slightly up. I assumed that this was due to the
high altitude, and in consequence kept very quiet for a day
or two. As it never rose over a hundred, I soon grew tired
of resting, and bought myself some racket snowshoes, so
that I could leave the cleared paths and walk over the
mountains. On one of these excursions, I descended a steep
slope, to come suddenly upon a bright fire, built by a band
of woodcutters, its scarlet flames flickering against the
whiteness of the snow like a tattered cardinal's robe upon
a field of ermine. Flames and snow, and strong bearded
men, sitting, like characters in one of Grimm's fairy-stories,
under the shadows of the pine trees.

On another day I went with pretty Imogen to look for

the grave of a friend of hers, dead three years before. It would have interested Theodore, I thought, to have seen me scrabbling in the snow, trying in vain to find a headstone with the name of my rival carved upon it. How cold it was, scraping at that frozen surface, but not so cold, I'll be bound, as it felt in the frozen earth below! I had a letter from Theodore that evening. 'I am delighted to hear that all goes well; but don't fall off one of those bloody mountains. Your wisdom grows here; it fell upon good ground. Joy *is* never-ending; only it must be the joy that dares to drink to the bottom. Talk of cold! Verily my bones freeze, and all water is ice. How the wind shakes the chain on my coach-house door. "I have never been sick or sorry," was a word I heard, to-day, said with pride. "Neither wilt thou be," I might have added, "until thou beginnest to live." '

One day I went on a long excursion with Imogen. We had our luncheon seated behind a châlet, she sitting on a milk-stool that I found half buried in the snow, and I on a board. It was warm in the sun, and the air about the old wooden shelter was fragrant with the mountain hay upon which we had been playing, and which was piled high up in the dim aromatic interior of that upland barn. I looked with glee at the dry, brown, dung-stained wood on which I sat, at the two empty shells of the hen's eggs, which my companion said I must bury, and at the sea-green icicles, which hung from a mountain-precipice, far up above us, like frozen snot on a giant's beard. And then I coughed, and recognised the unmistakable taste of mortality, and fear leapt in my throat like a live frog. Imogen had been very charming

G

to me that morning. When we finally left the hut, I gave her the hare's foot which I had got from Willie as a cure against any fresh attack of the stone. 'Ah! now,' she said laughing, 'I shall be able to run swiftly to you, or swiftly away from you, just as I want'; and her free eyes mocked at me, with challenging mischief, from under her hair, which was the exact colour of faded bracken seen with the sun upon it.

When we reached the road, we followed behind a line of sleighs, the drivers brandishing long whips by the sides of their jangling teams. We stopped at a wayside house, and two old women brought us milk in white china cups. They stood by us in amazement, and one of them put out her hand and touched Imogen's hair. Within the house was a man in a blue smock, dipping bread into a steaming bowl.

Presently we left, and once more tramped up the slippery road. It began to snow, and our footsteps made two parallel tracks. How curious, I thought, to consider one's physical progress over the face of the earth. In my mind's eye, as we climbed higher and higher, I seemed to see the movement of each individual, of each human being, like the shining, silvery paths of so many snails over an enormous rhubarb-leaf. For from the moment that our voices are first heard, from the moment that we begin to clutch, with wrinkled fingers, strong as the claws of a paroquet, and yet dainty as ivory bobbins, until such time as we are laid away in hollow coffins, it must be remembered that we actually make a physical progress, to and fro, this way and that, through cities, over mountains, through forests, over deserts, in and out of my lady's chamber, past this or that field-gate, advancing, doubling back, like hunted foxes, some to be run to earth in the home covert, and others in forests and quarries, far enough removed from the place of their birth.

We approached Arosa by the lower valley. For some distance our way lay near the river. It was melancholy to see how befouled it had become; everywhere, on its banks, heaps of refuse, from which, at intervals, hideous crows flapped away, calling, 'Cark! Cark! Cark!'

Imogen had taken off her glove to push her hair more securely under her hat. I caught her bare hand and held it fast. It was tremulous and warm, like a live thrush.

CHAPTER FIFTEEN

'Nay . . . Very Red'

THE NEXT morning, after breakfast, I had occasion to speak to my friend, the gold-braided porter. As we were talking, my eyes strayed over a large map of the Engadine, which hung on the wall behind his ponderous head. Suddenly they were arrested by the words, 'Davos Platz', in close juxtaposition to that of Arosa. Immediately I examined the map more closely, and discovered, to my extreme surprise, that although by train the two places were separated by a twenty-four-hour journey, as the crow flies, only some fifteen or twenty miles of mountain lay between them. And what was more, I realised that the mountain at which I had so often looked from the hotel verandah was nothing else than the topmost ridge of 'Queen Victoria in Bed', as seen from 'the other side'. This discovery, so unexpected, amazed and fascinated me. I became haunted now by a mountain that rose beyond the river, the same mountain over which, in the map, were written the words Furka Pass. I could think of nothing else but that so short a distance lay between me and the well-known scenes of my long illness. It was like one of those dreams, when familiar places, far distant from each other, are suddenly, to one's utter astonishment, found to converge, when the school-yard of Acreman House, for instance, would be found suddenly, unaccountably, to open into the

poplar-field behind Hocky's House. That morning's discovery seemed now completely to obsess my imagination.
I would be forever looking up at the Furka Pass and at the
mountain which rose behind it. The people with whom I
had made friends interested me now not a jot. Even when
I was out with sweetest Imogen, I would be preoccupied.
A strange madness seemed to have fallen upon me, such as
I conjecture seizes upon cats when they feel suddenly compelled to return to the place from whence they came. I
kept imagining myself descending those very slopes whose
beauty, as seen from my bed with the last glow of the hot
sun upon them, had so often beguiled for me the end of a
long afternoon. Eventually, I determined, come what might,
I would try to cross the mountains.

The day I selected for my adventure was cloudless. I
told no one of my purpose. I walked slowly, but steadily,
and soon found myself above the timber line. Here I was
confronted by smooth sheets of sparkling, virginal snow.
The crows in the dark trees below croaked a warning, but
I gave no heed to them. The actual Furka Pass, as I remember
it, was about two hundred yards wide. It was a steep incline
of snow that went down into I knew not what abyss. I un-
strapped my snowshoes. By stamping with my boots I found
I was able to break the frosty crust of the snow, and in this
way secure a firm footing.

Once over the pass, I was on the edge of a long mountain-
plateau, surrounded by high peaks. All was glittering white.
All was silent. No track of man or animal traversed that
high expanse. No flight of bird cleft its blue rarefied air,

Only one living thing did I meet—a tortoiseshell butterfly! It came fluttering towards me, over those eternal snows, with the aimless, careless flight that seems characteristic of this particular species. All the time I kept looking up at the sky. I knew my real danger lay in the possibility of being overtaken by a snow-storm. On I went, over the level stretches of that high No Man's Land. And ever behind me I left a peculiar, webbed track, as though some fabulous grebe had come waddling over the mountains. I was excited. I felt my pulse. It was racing. As the hours passed I became more and more conscious of the hot flush of my sickness tingling under my skin. Half stifled by the palpitations of my heart, I walked on. Shadows purple and drunken lay across the snow; while above me, so close that I staggered under it like a man who fears to lift his head, glowered the flaming orb of the azygous sun.

And then, suddenly, all my misgivings vanished, and I was rewarded. I had reached the last ridge, and, behold, I was looking down on the Frauenkïrch valley! There, far below, on the slope of the mountain opposite, stood the sanatorium, like a tiny, trig doll's house against the stupendous Alpine landscape. I was exultant. I was in an ecstasy. I knew that I was actually standing on one of the very ridges that had seemed to me only the year before as remote as the farthest rose-cupped cloud. For a time I could find no way by which I could reach the timber-line below. Then, by skirting along the edge of a dangerous-looking snow-field, I at last arrived at the trees. I found a mountain shed, with a woodcutter's path leading from it. Half an hour afterwards

I was in the Frauenkïrch village. I hired a room in the little inn, and made my way slowly up to the sanatorium, not forgetting to stop for a moment at the white mill to touch with my fingers the place where the plaster had broken off in the shape of a dromedary.

I arrived at the sanatorium just as the patients were collecting in the dining-room. My appearance seemed miraculous, my story unbelievable. With my face tanned to an unhealthy, blazing red, I walked from one familiar group to another, the young German doctor, in his white coat, following me about, asking me, in broken English, to explain how I had cured myself. And all the while, as I was receiving their congratulations, I could feel an impediment in my breathing, and my heart knocking against the walls of my ribs like the rattling beat of some cheap alarum-clock. Before long I left the noisy hall and stepped into the cold snow outside, illuminated, as of old, by reflections from those sad, flaunting windows. On the way back I entered a mountain forest. What was that I heard, as I crouched there, on the hard snow, dibbled with fallen twigs and fir-cones—the scuffling of the hounds of death?

When I reached the inn I went straight to bed. By throwing open the double windows, I flooded my room with frosty air. I lay down, but I could not sleep. Nervous thoughts scurried through my skull like mice in an attic. Once, twice, three times, I heard the pre-reformation bell in the little timber church strike the hour; and then, all at once, I began to suspect that what I had half been anticipating had actually happened. With a miserable sinking at the pit of my stomach I suddenly recognised the intolerable bubbling sensation in my chest, indicative of a hæmorrhage. I turned on the light, hoping against hope. I coughed; I looked; and once more I saw blood!

Slowly, very slowly, the dawn came. News of my relapse was sent to my old doctor, and a sleigh arrived, a black, closed sleigh, to carry me back to the sanatorium, the greatest fool in all that dolorous citadel. Once more I lay on my back, perfectly motionless, like a rabbit who 'freezes' in a thicket of thorns, in the hope that he will not be seen, in the hope that the danger that threatens him will pass by. Once more I was waked each morning by the clinking sound of sputum cups being collected in the white corridor outside. Once more I was looking out beyond the shadowed contours of 'Queen Victoria in Bed' to where the pale-green light of the evening sky, pale-green as the wing of a katydid, spoke in so deceptive, in so deceitful a manner of the immortality of the soul.

THE VERDICT
OF BRIDLEGOOSE

Dedicated

to

Edna St. Vincent Millay

a leprechaun

among poets

I OBSERVE, GENTLEMEN, in this Bridlegoose, several things, which induce me to represent before you, that it is my opinion that he should be pardoned. In the first place, his old age. Secondly, his simplicity. To both which qualities our statute and common laws, civil and municipal together, allow many excuses for any slips or escapes, which, through the invincible imperfection of either, have been inconsiderately stumbled upon by a person so qualified. Thirdly, gentlemen, I must needs display before you another case, which in equity and justice, maketh much for the advantage of Bridlegoose; to wit, that this one, sole, and single fault of his ought to be quite forgotten, abolished and swallowed up by that immense and vast ocean of just awards and sentences which heretofore he hath given and pronounced; his demeanour, for these forty years and upwards, that he hath been a judge, having been so evenly balanced in the scales of uprightness, that envy itself, till now, could not have been so impudent as to accuse and twit him with any act worthy of a check or reprehension. As, if a drop of the sea were thrown into the Loire none could perceive, or say, that, by this single drop, the whole river should be salt and brackish.

The third book of Rabelais' Works

CHAPTER ONE

Discontent

NEVER HAD I experienced a deeper discontent than I felt in my father's house at Weymouth after my return from Africa. Suddenly I found myself deprived of the two principal props upon which human happiness depends—work and love. I had escaped from the shores of Lake Elmenteita in the hope that I should be able to make a fresh start at writing; but how could I call it writing, this perpetual concentration upon manuscripts that were never published? Whenever I took up my pen a heavy melancholy weighed me down. 'Had not I, in my time, heard lions roar?' The consciousness that I had escaped from my labours merely to discover myself edged into the position of an ineffectual literary dilettante filled me with disgust. Indeed, so obsessed did I grow with the sense of my personal futility that I even became indifferent to the simple and beautiful glimpses of life that surrounded me on every side. I, the lover of life, the son of the sun, became a renegade and remained unmoved before what I had always held most dear. In the autumn, as I passed Lodmoor, I would see the fishermen drawing their nets out of the sea, and walk on inattentive. The sight of the cormorants, flying with outstretched necks toward the wave-washed promontories near the White Nore, meant nothing to me; the colour of the rushes in the dykes, lit up by the last rays of the sun as it went down behind the Chesil beach, nothing; the winter stars shining at midnight upon the backs of Dorset sheep, asleep on Dorset downs, less than nothing.

I do not think, however, that I would have been foolish enough to have allowed my hurt vanity to work this ill upon me had I been in a position to draw happiness from that other great human consolation, but to be denied all amorous delights! When I was dressing I would look into the mirror and see tiny wrinkles about my eyes and grey hairs appearing over my temples, and this would throw me into a mood of the deepest dejection. It was as though in that neat bathroom, so white, so compact, so well-appointed, God had all at once taken it into His head to give me a tip, to whisper into my ear that I had no time to waste. Of course I realised perfectly well the cause of my predicament. Nothing else, in fact, than that it was my misfortune to belong to, to have been born into, the English middle class. For after all, what a terrible class it is; merely to have occasional intercourse with the people who belong to it is awful enough, but to be born one of them! It is like finding oneself in an enormous wire trap unable to get out. You can get in; anybody can get in, *but you can't get out*. I used to lie in my bed in torment, and during these midnight vigils it would seem to me that amorous dalliance was the one thing that mattered in life, that the complete and utter gratification of one's most lively whim was, in truth, the only real and abiding good to be found on earth. And then I would reflect that the bulls with brass rings in their noses, the stallions with bands round their bellies, were in better case than I. Why, the very sparrows in the gutter, the very mice squealing and romping in the wainscot-tunnels of my father's house, were refreshed a thousand times more often. On many an evening during that summer, as I sat smoking after dinner at the open window while the table was being cleared of the brittle red remnants of the lobsters that had just been eaten, I would suffer an agony of jealousy as I watched boys and girls in a never-ending stream pass to and fro along the esplanade. I would find myself intensely, exquisitely sensitive to the pulse and rhythm of life, and yet know all the while that by some wretched cast of the dice I was doomed to remain, perforce, outside, like a sheep with a splash of tar on its tail, who is not allowed to mix with the flock. And all the time there would come in, through the open window, that enervating seaside smell, suggestive of rattling egg-shaped pebbles, of painted row-boats lying bottom upwards, of tennis-shoes made warm by the delicate sandy feet of young girls. I used certainly to undergo very strange inarticulate emotions by that wide-open bow window, emotions that would seem to acquire something of the eternal, and yet be contained in the short space of time that lay between the removal of the lobster-shells and the brushing away of the crumbs.

In July, I went to Southampton to meet my brother John, who was returning from the United States for a holiday. As we sat together on the wharf he asked me whether I would not consider going back with him to America. I answered without hesitation that I would go back with him. Had not I been feeling for the last twelve-month that it was high time for me to be setting out on my travels again, to be setting out on my travels for a new jungle? I had no mind to remain any longer under my father's protection, cooped up like a prize hen. I would rather starve, I thought, in a garret of New York city, than live so mean a life.

CHAPTER TWO

Tentative Overtures

I SET SAIL for America with the vaguest idea as to what I intended to do. I had lost every penny I possessed from investments in German marks. My plans for the future were most fanciful. Sometimes I imagined that I might become a salesman, sometimes I dreamed of success in business through the influence of some benevolent magnate. It seemed quite obvious that I could never hope to make a living out of writing. How could I expect to do so when all that I wrote remained unpublished?

Of course, my best chance of earning a livelihood lay in taking up some kind of scholastic employment; but then I hated teaching, and accepted it as a good omen when my Cambridge cap and gown and woolly bachelor's hood, which I had strapped to the outside of my Gladstone bag, were lost at the dock on my landing.

My brother and sister lived at this time in an apartment on Twenty-first Street, opposite the Theological Seminary, and it was here that I stayed for six months, endeavouring, as best I might, to adapt myself to my new environment.

Not long after my arrival I visited an employment agent in the down-town section of New York. It was with a feeling of extreme trepidation that I found myself one afternoon moving through the shadowed canyons of this part of the city. I felt as lost and terrified as an ant might feel, which, fallen from the basket of a Sunday 'hiker', finds itself advancing over a grassless, mouldless floor, without hope of sustenance or friendly shelter. At last I reached the office I sought. It was at the top of an enormous building. After waiting in a queue for half an hour my turn came to be interviewed. I said that I wanted any kind of work. A competent young man with well-brushed hair regarded me for a moment with an assessing eye. He asked me for my past history. I told him that I had taken a degree at Cambridge and had been a stock-rancher in East Africa. 'I am sorry we can do nothing for you,' he said, and nodded to the man behind me, who was already, with nervous, trembling fingers, taking from his pocket certain papers. I went out of the door feeling that my current value was exactly nothing. The corridor outside was empty, and my sense of incompetence was still further augmented by the fact that I had no idea what to do to persuade the elevator to stop and carry me away from the long, deserted gallery which I found so unspeakably depressing. Once I saw a red light glow out above one of the prison-gates, but before I had time to reach it the descending cage had disappeared smoothly and rapidly into an alarming hollow depth.

It was after this experience that I seriously considered accepting a job offered me by a firm of Philadelphia undertakers. I knew that in Africa the task of consorting with the dead was allocated to the lowest pariahs; and as my value in America seemed exactly nought, it appeared to be an occupation to which I might with some show of justification aspire. Besides, how the profession would jump with my abnormal preoccupation with all matters that have to do with mortality, and what philosophic insight I might gain into the wild, quivering, uncertain manners of life as I paid midnight visits to each new 'silent room of sorrow'! Long afterwards, whenever I walked down Eighth Avenue, past my savings bank, past the three golden balls of Uncle Ben's pawn-shop, my attention would always be arrested by the illuminated words, *Stephen Merritt, Undertaker*. And when I came abreast of the establishment I could never resist peering into the dark recesses of the sober, heavily carpeted room, where, at a polished desk, furnished with a telephone, under a bearded bust that suggested the head of Æschylus, sat a representative of the firm awaiting the next call. And as I continued on my way along the crowded, garish street, I would half persuade myself that I envied this black-befrocked gentleman, who, with his feet resting on an ebony ottoman, appeared to be reading, with such absorbed attention, Shirlock upon death. For night and day, as I walked these crowded thoroughfares, I would scan with astonishment the faces of the citizens of New York City, citizens who always appeared so busily employed, so capable, and so prosperous. How did it come about, I wondered, that all these people possessed the faculty of adapting themselves to the requirements of an age for the meanest demands of which I myself felt so entirely unfitted!

One afternoon, as I sauntered up Fifth Avenue, engaged in this favourite pastime, each new set of features presenting itself to my attention, insistent and emphatic, only to disappear a moment later into an unchartered oblivion, like the masks of so many quick souls passing like butterflies to a frivolous doom, some very queer and very shameless imaginings entered my head. I would be perfectly willing, I thought, to accept the most ambiguous position in the world in the households of some of these charming women, if by such means I could receive a dole of bread and butter. Hardly had this ingenuous reflection taken up its abode in my head, in the head of a simple countryman who knows exactly how to find the nest of a false lapwing, or how to extract a rabbit from its hole with a bramble, than I received a sharp cut across my face, as though some omniscient moralist had struck me with a wire whip, and I awoke from my equivocal dreams to realise that I had collided with an energetic Jew and had sent his sharp-edged straw hat rolling like a quoit across the sidewalk. This encounter took place exactly opposite the Public Library, exactly opposite the place where those two lions are couched, who, with simpering, complacent expressions so different from any expressions I have observed on the countenance of any real lion, contemplate with unshut eye, for ever and aye, the strutting, artificial figures that pass before them.

It was now that somebody gave me a letter of introduction to a celebrated journalist. I went to see him, nursing the hope that as he was an Englishman, and a graduate of John's College, Cambridge, he might put me in the way of doing some literary work. I timidly knocked at the door of his office, a door that had his name printed upon it, and

entered to find a tall, good-natured, heavily built man, in
shirt sleeves, sitting at a desk. He had at one time been a
member of Parliament, in the Liberal interest, and had
since been making a living by writing gossipy articles about
well-known English politicians, the information that he
was in a position to impart, and his method of imparting it,
being exactly suited to the taste of the readers of the Magazine Sections of the more important New York newspapers.
Mr. ―― treated me with generous civility, asking me to
come and lunch with him at his club. During this meal I
was aware of being under *his* assessing eye, and when he
asked me as a test question, what I thought of the Irish
situation, and discovered that I thought nothing about it,
I was conscious, painfully conscious, as I ate my mutton-
chop, of his estimation of me having dropped very many
degrees. 'My advice to you, young man,' he said presently,
'is to go West.' It would be a mistake for the reader to
suppose that I myself had not been forming my own shy
conclusions about the character and taste of my host, as I
sat at the heavy mahogany table, and learnt how interested
Mr. ―― was in all that had to do with the life of our
Saviour, and listened to him chaffing his son, who was a
keen philatelist, about stamps 'simply adhering to him',
or indeed bandying cheerful jocularities with the door-
keeper as to the exact date when, by an unwritten law,
straw hats were supposed to disappear from the street. We
parted outside the club, and I never saw him again, though
for many years I used to read with no small envy his articles
on men and affairs and marvel to myself at his amazing

capacity for understanding and explaining each 'new situation' as it arose.

After this luncheon I returned to my brother's room. He at once did all he could to influence me toward trying to make a living in New York City by writing. 'Now that Mr. —— has told you to go West, I should most certainly make up my mind to stay East,' he said. However, I dare say I should never have tried to make my living by writing, if it had not been for Miss Mary Siegrist, who assured me that I would find no difficulty in doing so, going even so far as to give me a letter of introduction to Mr. Dounce, of the New York *Evening Post*. As the years passed I saw less and less of Mary Siegrist, but I never forgot the kindness she showed me at this critical juncture in my life, or feel anything but admiration for a certain lyrical quality in her poetry, a quality which can never be wholly destroyed, however assiduously she may associate herself with tiresome people and tiresome women's clubs. Armed with her letter I presented myself at the office of her friend. Mr. Dounce, a clever young man, treated me then, as always, with extreme courtesy, asking me to write some vignettes of Africa. The first sketch I wrote was entitled 'A Porcupine in a Kitchen', and I received for it just three dollars and seventy-five cents.

CHAPTER THREE

Herring-Gulls

FOR MY health's sake I used to sleep on the roof, carrying my blankets up through a trap-door. It would be a hard matter to convey how liberating to my spirit I found this practice to be. Life in a great, modern city can in an extraordinary way traduce one's mind into accepting as reality the illusion of each feverish, fleeting day, and it is only by having certain hours set apart for the persuasion of a more sensitive and profound consciousness that one can hope to keep one's soul clear. To emerge through a little trap-door to find myself alone with fresh night-wandering clouds, alone with the cozening moon and a myriad isolated stars never failed to restore my being to that fortunate state of awareness which alone would seem to justify our existence, in contrast with the existence of the beasts of the field. When it rained I would wake and go into the house, but when snow fell I would often continue to sleep, opening my eyes at dawn to find the old, dusty, crumbling chimneys, each one of which had become as familiar to me as the pear-trees in the back-yard at home, rising out of a little square lawn of unsmutched nativity snow. To return from some crowded drawing-room, where I had been listening, it may be, to Amy Lowell reading her poetry, reading 'Patterns', and to see, at the hour before the dawn, herring-gulls, one after the other, with deliberate flight, cross from horizon to horizon over the Island City, was to experience a most rare subjective release.

I remember well the particular party I have in mind—Amy Lowell enthroned on a high-backed chair, smoking her cigar and eyeing the company with the aggressive, narrow eye of some high-pedigreed bird, whose narrow head is large enough to contain only two thoughts, herself and her own expensive eggs. It always seemed to me that Miss Lowell's personality was far superior to her poetry. She had the kind of bad manners which by their effrontery become good manners. 'I am glad that you are not your brother,' she said to me that evening, when I was introduced to her. And, in truth, the difference between my brother John's nature, incalculable as the nature of a plumed 'serpent', and Amy Lowell's nature, so pectinated and emphatic, could hardly be exaggerated.

There were many people of interest at this particular gathering. Lola Ridge was there to read some of her verse, and it was amusing to watch the undisguised hauteur on the face of Miss Lowell, as she listened to the poetry of her rival. I had met Lola Ridge a few days before, in the rooms of Evelyn Scott, and both my brother and I had been impressed by the beauty of her face, like the impassive death-mask of a saint. Evelyn Scott kept green little paroquets in a hutch at the back of a darkened garret; and afterwards, when I read the writings of this gifted woman, I always associated these same paroquets, their testy temperaments and beaks sharp as darning-needles, with the bitter, nipping style of their attractive mistress. But for all my professed alertness I must have been singularly stupid and unobservant at this party; for while the recitations were taking place, there was sitting next to me, so I learnt afterwards, a very distinguished person, and one whose deep nature and exceptional ability I was, at a later time, to come to value highly indeed. As it was, I sat on a low divan, giving attention to everybody else. I observed Professor Crane and his wife. I always liked the Professor, and he was always kind to me, albeit it cannot be denied that in his critical writing he is a little inclined to balance himself with edifying adroitness on the fence. Behind the Professor sat Mr. Scofield Thayer, dressed immaculately, with his head resting on his hand, but at the same time tilted upward, so that I was able to catch a glimpse, against the delightful swan-like curve of a young girl's bare shoulder, of an expression, superb in its supercilious fastidiousness, as with immobile ivory features, he listened to what was being repeated. This young man came to represent for me, as I knew him better, a most admirable type of American. Courteous, cultured, illustrious, he seemed to suggest in each attitude he took, in each movement he made, that most fortunate state wherein the vulgar, material resources of the world have been compelled to minister, whether they like it or not, to every form of æsthetic expression. A little to the left of this incomparable arbiter, with his smile of indulgent disdain, sat Gaston La Chaise, the sculptor, whose sober carriage and handsome dark, clear-cut head made so interesting a contrast to the appearance and demeanour of his proud peacock wife, a woman capable of advancing down Eighth Street with the inspiring gait of an empress. Not far off sat Mr. Van Wyck Brooks, concentrated, alert, self-conscious, his curious wide-awake features surmounted by well currycombed schoolboy hair. I was speaking to him just before the party broke up, and we left the house together. As we turned the corner into Sixth Avenue he mentioned Amy Lowell's poetry. 'It is all right, but she is not really important,' he said; and as we made our way across the street under the elevated railway, I recollect feeling an immediate response to his words, a response of enthusiasm that there still remained certain custodians of literature who refuse to be gulled, though it is by a Boston magnate of poesy in her pleasure dome of sacrosanct violet-coloured glass. But let the soul of Amy Lowell rest in peace; in spite of all her failings, in spite of her solid silver candelabra, and her extraordinary publicity-sense, she was an imposing and gallant figure, and a great character of our time.

As I passed under the library of the Anglican Seminary that night, I remember coming upon one of those street incidents which are to me always so agitating. A man, apparently dead-drunk, was lying on the curb with an enormous policeman standing over him. In order to rouse him to consciousness I saw the officer deliberately strike him over the head two or three times with a rough piece of board which he had taken from a near-by garbage-tin. At each stroke the small crowd which had collected laughed that uneasy sycophantic laugh which foreigners in America are inclined to give when they come up against some crude example of Irish or Anglo-Saxon brutality. I was far too nervous to interfere and hurried on. When I did look round I saw that the drunkard had been revived and was leaning against a lamp-post, with blood streaming from his forehead. Such New York street adventures were always peculiarly painful to my nerves. On one occasion I saw a woman being taken to Jefferson Market Prison. Two constables were carrying her, and the one behind, who held her by the wrists, seemed to take deliberate satisfaction in allowing her grey hair to drag along the pavement. Indeed, as he looked round at the crowd, I caught an expression on his face of a kind of pride, the pride of an actor who is playing his part well and is providing the audience with the thrill they demand, and the audience, the human beings, who witnessed with me this particular act, what a curious, fatuous interest was displayed on their faces, the very same fatuous interest I had once noted on the countenances of a group of people whom I came upon watching the runnings to and fro of a mouse which, loose in the street, and with its small grey body covered with mud, was wildly and hopelessly trying to find some place of refuge from a publicity its instinct told it was fatal to its safety. It must be acknowledged that it is extremely hard to think of the human race as noble. One can only say that under certain circumstances certain individuals have upon occasion, acted with nobility; for the rest, without being actively malicious, we are only too prone to regard the harsh sequence of a cause and effect, the dragging prongs of the iron harrow with which the Devil harrows us, with a kind of base curiosity, the base curiosity of a set of booby-heads lolling over a fence to witness the roasting alive of a black cat.

But how lovely, after so many confused impressions, to be able to dissociate oneself entirely from one's fellow witlings, to be cognisant only of one's own arrant identity, dozing like a carrier pigeon on a sooty roof-top, asleep in a Universe whose unravished calm remains, and always will remain, unaffected by the too-clever inventions of Mr. Thomas A. Edison and his bright compatriots. Consider the effects upon one's spirits of a Socony Station, stained with oil, of the concentrated banality of radio-broadcasting, of automobiles and of the cement boulevards they traverse, and let us be grateful that though our kind can outrage the virginal surface of the earth, yea! and the pure atmosphere around it, with every kind of abomination, it is still incapable of tampering, even in the least degree, with the august progression of the moon; still less with the punctual bands of Orion!

CHAPTER FOUR

Poetry and Prejudice

IT WAS the first autumn I had spent in America; and as week followed week, and month followed month, with town and country bathed in a still spacious air, more tranquil, more pellucid, than I had known in Africa or Europe, I felt my appreciation of the New World rise ever higher. I knew the fogs and damp of an English autumn —who better? But now I realised I had come to a country where a large, gracious atmosphere transvalued all values. And this impression remained with me to the end. For, in spite of its aptitude for standardisation, its newspaper public opinion, in spite of all that is intolerable in this country of material revelations and mock idealism, it remains a land essentially disenthralled, where half the shackles cloying free movement have been broken, and where a certain casual nonchalant good-humour, tough as the rind of pumpkins, does reciprocate the spaciousness of the air. Weeks passed, and still the trees on the Palisades retained their autumn colouring under what to an Englishman seemed a cloudless mid-summer sky.

One afternoon, during that winter, I attended a lecture that my brother gave at a certain women's club. Before he spoke, the two hundred and fifty members who made up his audience all stood up and began to recite, like a set of Sunday-school children, a patriotic hymn, and at a given moment thrust out long arms in the direction of the American flag. I was, I must confess it, a trifle taken aback. Here was a gathering of women who were probably the leaders of society in this particular neighbourhood, and yet they apparently felt no misgiving at taking part in so provincial a display. When I considered the intellectual aridity, the lack of taste, capable of producing such a cere-mony upon such an occasion, I could only gasp. Yet the set expression on those female faces, as they pointed at the Stars and Stripes, just as savages might point at the totem of their tribe, has remained always in my memory, to remind me, when I grow unduly optimistic, of the unen-lightenment which lies like a miasmic mist in the way of any charming and tolerant civilisation. After the perform-ance was over, and we had escaped, we walked through a succession of streets, trying to find some opening that would give us a view over the wide New Jersey marshes. We could find no break, and as we walked past each com-pact birdcage of a house, I made reference to the depressing spectacle we had just witnessed. 'Oh, you need not worry about that,' said my brother. 'Those places are mere back-waters, dreary retreats for pathetic women. Another fifty years will see the end of clubs of that kind, its members will have been replaced by the young people, gay, healthy, and unscrupulous, whose laughter we hear in these streets.'

It was now that there fell into my hands, for the first time, the poetry of Edna St. Vincent Millay. There was something about these lyrics, these snatches of song, con-

tained in the slim black volume called *Renascence*, that
amazed and enchanted me. They seemed to express a spirit
at once daring and sensitive, and to possess a beauty which
however slight, was separate and authentic as only true
poetry can be.

Late that autumn I managed to procure an introduction
to her. She lived in a house on Twelfth Street, which has
since been demolished, but which was then owned by a
certain Mrs. Helmar, a competent, good-natured little
Irishwoman, who could be extraordinarily indulgent to the
lodgers she liked, and extraordinarily mean to those she
disliked. I mounted the steps and rang the bell three times,
as I had been directed to do. Presently I found myself in
the presence of the girl I so much honoured. Her appearance in no way disappointed me. She was dainty with a
daintiness that can only be compared with the daintiness
of Queen Anne's lace or with the daintiness of a spider-
web gossamer such as I have seen decorating the leaves
of dahlia flowers on a September morning. It is true that I
did detect in her look an April shadow of vanity, but
below this self-conscious protection was a living represen-
tation of the divine spirit of poetry, uncontaminated as the
spirit of Catullus, gay as the spirit of John Suckling. I never
became disillusioned; the more I saw of this young and
most beautiful girl, the more I came to appreciate the rash
quality of her nature, heedless and lovely as a fieldfare
rising from the wintry ground. She might disguise herself
in all the pretty frippery that she could buy at Wanamaker's,
she might be photographed for *Vanity Fair* every day of the

week, and yet below her laces and ribbons there will always remain a barefoot poet, doomed yet redeemed, under the shadow of Eternity.

Of course, it cannot be gainsaid that *Vanity Fair* has been responsible for influencing, not always for the better, the literary styles of many gifted writers. The paper prides itself on publishing the work of the most distinguished men and women of our time; and because of the high rates that it pays it becomes a temptation, apparently even to people of sound talent, to adapt themselves to the smart tone that this fashionable journal especially favours. In my lean days I myself have been eager enough to be given an opportunity to succumb to such a temptation; but because of the difficulty of converting a piece of ground-ivy into a hothouse plant, my name has only once appeared in the paper, and this on the occasion when Mr. Crowninshield magnanimously published a purely propagandist piece of writing against motion picture films of wild life in Kenya Colony which had struck me as more than usually stupid and brutal. I was entertained, when I called at the office, by Mr. Edmund Wilson, the scholarly and sagacious critic whose work we have all come to admire so much. On seeing him I wondered how he could ever have permitted himself and his friend, Mr. John Peale Bishop, to select for a volume of poems, some of which were written in a mood of serious philosophic pessimism, so ill-chosen a title as *An Undertaker's Garland*, being altogether oblivious, apparently, of the deep offence inherent in such felicitous facetiousness. One longs for the formidable voice of some great ancient divine—

some Dr. John Donne or some Jeremy Taylor—to thunder out at these young elegants. You can write of life with bitterness, nay, with intemperate ferocity, and all is well, but surely triviality should be reserved for the trivial. The secret of existence is deep, and again deep, and it is never pleasant to hear superficial society voices in moments of vision or emotional stress. Consider the desperate nature of the terms upon which we live, consider life's savagery and beauty, the infinite variety of the Creator's harvested imagination, the lark bounding higher and higher into the sky, the dainty horned snail carrying with deliberate purpose its convoluted shell through grass-stems; consider the deadly brevity of our days, with evil connecting us together like a terrible live-wire, and then contemplate death, that final, abominable subterfuge, which at a single blow reduces everything to nothing. Contemplate the look on a young girl's face who supports on her knees the head of her dead lover, and then surely it will be revealed how these young men of fashion blundered from an æsthetic point of view.

Before Mr. Wilson appeared, I sat for some minutes in the waiting-room, watching, perhaps not altogether honestly, a succession of young girls pass by the door. The offices of *Vanity Fair* certainly possessed a tone, an atmosphere, peculiar to themselves. As one glanced at the clever, snappy faces passing backwards and forwards along the carpeted corridors, faces that looked so admirably adapted to modern life, one could not help being reminded of Miss Nancy Boyd's prose style. (Ah, what a fall is there!) Indeed, these smart maidens, with their weasel waists and high-heeled morocco slippers, appeared to be perfect products of the magazine whose interests they served. After I had talked a few minutes with Mr. Wilson, a point arose over which it seemed judicious to consult Mr. Crowninshield, and I was admitted into the presence of the great man. Mr. Crowninshield was wearing a modish coat of a superb cut, and had the air of a competent and polite man of the world who had somehow or other managed to combine the efficient look of an alert business magnate with the superb nonchalance of the manager of some exclusive seaside hotel—in short, a kind of Beau Nash of Park Avenue!

That year on Christmas Eve there was a heavy fall of snow. It came fluttering down from far up in the heavens, upon the pavements, upon the policemen directing the traffic, and upon the innumerable parcels that were distributed by the expressmen. I sat over a log-fire reading an ancient legend which told how a village idiot who was serving a priest on Christmas morning suddenly fell dead at the window 'where the saints stand in a row. For the face he had seen pressed against the coloured glass had ensnared his life as the fowler ensnared the supple neck of a bird with an invisible silken thread.'

Late in the evening I went to a party in the rooms of Mr. Conroy, the actor. Clare Eames was there, with her proud head held high amid wreathed fumes of tobacco and wine, and Mr. Sidney Howard also, tough, well-constituted, and not easy to shift. On the floor near the sofa gracefully reclined Mr. Rollo Peters, whose airy manner and light aristocratic touch roused in my over-grave countryman's

soul an obscure jealousy. The gathering was a gay one, the
punch was strong, the cherries well sugared, but for some
reason I felt sullen and out of it. I left with Edna St. Vincent
Millay, conducting her across Fifth Avenue. In a near-by
churchyard stood a spick-and-span Christmas tree, with
electric bulbs for candles. I looked askance at it, and yet,
though the lights were electric lights, it did help to suggest
the spirit of the season as I had known it at home in Dorset,
where at that very hour the lights from the cottage windows
of East Chaldon were, I knew, shining out into the darkness, visible as far away as the steep downland sheep-track
which leads you past where the broken harrow stands.

CHAPTER FIVE

Going West

ONE EVENING as I was returning from a party at Professor Crane's I became aware of a curious tingling sensation which soon developed into a severe attack of the grippe, and for several days I lay in bed with a high fever. Mrs. Hunt, with an untiring benevolence characteristic of her, came across each day from her home in the Seminary opposite, bringing me savoury dishes. It was through her that I afterwards met Winston Churchill, that good man who only quite recently has come to understand that the pavements of New York City and the grassy plots of Turtle Bay are not as solid as he had at first supposed. I could see Mrs. Hunt's square stone house from my window, and by placing a milk bottle in a certain position on my sill was able to signal to her when in any kind of distress. I could see other things from my window also, for on the opposite side of the Seminary lawns stood several boarding houses patronised by stenographers; and nothing would give me more pleasure during the evenings of my convalescence than to watch these pretty young ladies throw off their frocks when they came in from work. I was indeed enchanted by the glimpses I got of their slim, white, naked figures moving to and fro in their bedrooms with the provoking unconsciousness of half a dozen rare birds, whose characteristic plumage, as they flit from twig to twig, one cannot observe quite as clearly as one would like to do.

It was now decided that for my health's sake I should visit California with my brother. I was to meet him in Chicago. I stopped over at Niagara Falls. It was here that I saw my first American robin, strutting about over a patch of fresh green grass on Goat Island. I recollect admiring its proud, light gait, that particular springtime gait which Alfeo Faggi, the sculptor, told me inspired him to model his Eve, one of the most beautiful of his statues.

I arrived in Chicago the next morning, to find my brother in bed at the Stratford Hotel. I sat by the window, while he dressed. It was a wet morning and the air was so full of mist that I could not see the lake. Up from underground came a never-ending stream of people. 'Clerks,' my brother said, 'coming in for their day's work.' 'Why don't they run away?' I asked. For even though I knew the pressure of necessity as well as another it seemed incredible to me that anybody in his senses could submit to so sordid a subjugation.

By the afternoon we had reached Fort Madison. I liked the look of this place. But what a river! I could see the dirty-yellow silt in its water as I peered down at it through the planks of the bridge over which our train rattled; and the dead, drowned trees on its banks, surely they had never budded or borne leaves? The next morning I waked at dawn. As soon as I had drawn up the green curtain, I found myself looking out on a dismal landscape. Along the distant horizon I saw continual flashes of lightning, zigzagging down to earth. In one homestead, dimly visible over a wide stretch of land, a light was shining; and as I was carried forward, I experienced a very definite sense of loss, in that I could never hope to have knowledge of the savour of the lives of the people who inhabitated the well-used rooms of that isolated abode. A day or two later the train began to cross the deserts of Arizona, flushed dog-rose, olive-green deserts, fading away to distant mountains. What kind of a god held sway in such a land? Some gilded-toed finicking Peruvian deity playing all day long with his own mincing shadow; though it appeared to be a most primitive country composed, perhaps, of chemical atoms less loaded with gravitation than other segments of the earth. One could imagine William Blake walking here naked, holding high converse with Los. The soil itself, light and painted, seemed to partake of the nature of the elements, as though by a belated creation it had been spared the blood-stained history of the Old World. We might, I thought, have been passing over the surface of Uranus or some other remoter planet, where there had been no fall, and consequently no need of salvation. Now and again we saw a flock of sheep, or some cattle, or a single horseman, and then again more plains, and more mountains, tawny and spotted as though huge cheetah-skins had been thrown across them. Some of the plains must have measured fifty or sixty miles from end to end, vast playing fields, where heroes and immortals might disport themselves with no fear but that there would be room for their castes. We crossed the Colorado River in the evening. Its banks were covered with masses of green foliage; and, looking behind us, we saw the bare, jagged Needle Rocks, forming a background suitable to some fantastic El Greco picture. The next morning, when we awoke, we were really in California. On each side of the track were green fields, grown with corn, already in full ear. Flowers were everywhere. Here was a cultivated land where the rougher usages of the stock-farmer had given place to gentler occupations, to the pruning of orchards, to the tending of vineyards, to the growing of corn. The railway track itself was overgrown with weeds and grasses, pushing their way up between the 'sleepers'. From above, the sun kept pouring down upon us, as we sat in the observation car, the air heavy with the smell of the secret fertility of the earth. By noon that day we were crossing the ferry to San Francisco; and standing on the deck, in the bright sunshine, I looked out through the Golden Gate, for the first time, at the Pacific.

We took rooms in a hotel at Sausalito, pleasant rooms that overlooked a garden. My brother, however, had no great liking for the place. The servants of the hotel were Filipinos; and as day followed day, he developed a definite antipathy for these little dark-eyed men in white clothes, who looked as if their 'bones were filled with air', and who would torment him in a thousand ways—by jangling on guitars, by gambling clink, clink, clink, outside our window, and by putting before him each meal-time a platter full of half-cooked carrots. I think they resented his being a vegetarian, and indeed found his personality peculiarly exasperating, the personality of this extraordinary man who had the appearance of one of their own heathen idols. For several days my brother would appear to be happy, and then once more the shrill, inhuman cries of these dapperlings would get on his nerves, and he would begin pacing up and down like a secretive, lean badger which finds itself trapped on a concrete floor with no chance of burrowing.

But we had certain golden moments. After our breakfast of pale cereal, served with thin milk, it became a habit with us to walk upon a high, terraced road flecked with the flickering shadows of eucalyptus trees. We were happy together.

We used to see a great deal of Sarah Bard Field and Colonel Wood, the former spirited and generous, and able to wear, prettily enough, flowers in her grey hair, the latter like some magnificent old chieftain, victor of a hundred battles. The knob of the electric bell on their front door had been sadly worn by the fingers of a procession of indigent poets and hungry radicals, but never was their bounty exhausted. Truly it was a noble thing to see the old man busy himself with the simples that he was preparing for a salad, or to follow behind him as he walked up Chinatown, white-haired, debonair, and bowed down with parcels. His ways are not my ways, his beliefs are not my beliefs; but I cannot but do homage to this old, unrelenting, white-maned lion of Oregon.

CHAPTER SIX

San Francisco

ONE DAY my brother and I walked to the sea. It was not a happy excursion. The beach appeared drab and littered. Whether it had ever possessed salt-washed, gleaming pebbles and yellow corrugated sands, I cannot say. That morning we found its margin made up of cinders and tattered pieces of paper and, what was worse still, cast-off automobile tires. Few objects in the world are capable of affecting my mind more unpleasantly than these derelict rings of india-rubber. One can imagine some limbo of cast-away objects in which old arrow heads, old spade handles, old sea wreckage, and the broken limbs of old dolls, would draw away in eternal disgust from these repulsive appendages of highways that are no highways.

We returned to our habitation among the Filipinos completely discouraged. The walk had evidently been too much for me, for the next morning I woke with an attack of blood-spitting. As always, this indication that I had again been overtaken by my vigilant enemy filled me with gloomy foreboding. That day it happened that my brother met George Sterling in the streets of San Francisco. This admirable Poet Laureate of the West, for whom we both felt so great a regard, on hearing of my predicament, did all in his power to persuade me to undergo treatment at Dr. Abrams' clinic.

Well do I remember walking up Sacramento Street toward the house of this Faustus of the twentieth century, with George Sterling at my side, his delicately moulded head marking him out as a poet, as the skylark is known by its tufted crest. In truth, I felt as I turned to look at his profile as though I were passing over the cobbled streets, not of San Francisco, but of Florence, and had at my side none other than Dante himself, but a Dante with two lusty horns protruding from his forehead like those to be seen in the head of Michael Angelo's Moses. For there was always something sportive and pagan about George Sterling; and when he told me it was a common pastime of his to dive for water-lilies in the ponds of Golden Gate Park, I felt in no way surprised. It seemed an occupation singularly appropriate to him, far more appropriate, indeed, than that he should select to stay at the Bohemian Club, that ostentatious resort of the rich business men of the city, who, each year, with a hundred and one flunkeys, betake themselves to the redwood forests for their 'high-jinks', a festival that any authentic poet, philosopher, or man of letters would shy away from as though it were an assembly of devils.

Dr. Abrams fascinated me. To this day I am confident that the man had a kind of mad genius. He was just one more of these bearded Jews, whose burning eyes scorch great holes in the manifold curtains that blind and stifle the human race. One felt that he was a Jacob who, while he wrestled with the angel from sunset to sunrise, kept glancing every half-hour at the oil-stove in the mouth of his tent upon

which his pottage was cooking. He had a nervous, pene-
trating glance. Sterling told me that he never allowed any
one to walk behind him. He certainly never rested; and I
used to like to think of him, all night long, unveiling, under
the shadow of the majestic Californian night-sky, a hundred
subtle secrets. I like quacks. I feel sympathetic toward
them and believe in them. On my soul, I'd as soon see an
honest Nic Culpeper at my bedside as half a dozen doctors
with their heads stuffed full of academic ewe's wool!

Abrams took a drop of blood from my left ear, meanwhile
making me stand in just such a position so that, as I looked
at the pretty figure of the uniformed nurse who held the
cotton-wool, my body would come into some cunning
harmony with the spinning movement of the earth as it
turned and turned like a green pea in a crystal ball. And
after he had found that I suffered from tuberculosis, and
by means of some dangling plummet of his own contrivance
had diagnosed (and he did this correctly) just exactly where
my sickness was still active, he set me down in front of his
electrical machine, and having already painted my right
shoulder-blade with some brilliant marsh-marigold yellow,
which after a few days formed a kind of shellac, he tied
under it a round-shaped battery, causing my flesh to tingle
as if the fin of a seal had been placed against it. I received
ten treatments. Every day I sat opposite the magic box with
a new patient; and on these occasions, when we were left
alone in the room, I was able to question each one as to
the success of the new remedy. They were enthusiastic
believers in the new treatment. They had known the deaf

to hear, the blind to see, and the halt to walk! At the end of ten days, I underwent a new blood-test and was pronounced cured. For two years I had no further trouble with my consumption. Dr. Abrams refused to take any money from me.

And now that the miracle had happened, and I was once again well, I took counsel with myself how I might best employ my time. I made many friends, but the one I loved best was Nan. She was an extraordinarily sweet-natured girl and suffered from no inhibitions whatever. To this day the memory of her gay laughter fills me with joy. A few hours of her company had the effect of ridding my own mind of I know not how many mean moralities. For after all, if you find a resting-place in some golden, ungarnered corn-field, with clinging bindweed and drugging red poppies and honey-bees all about you, it is hard to remain an artful, calculating, and ignoble renegade to your more spontaneous nature. How charming were the hours we spent together! One night we loitered long after the sun had gone down, in Golden Gate Park, sporting under the great trees, entranced by the beauty of the moonlight. 'For shame! I believe we are in the buffalo-pen,' she cried out once, in alarm; but I held her close and stroked her hand, which was as white as the hand of Izaak Walton's milkmaid. And looking up through the spreading branches at the stars, at the thousand and one cat's eyes, cold and crafty, I could not but marvel at the utter folly—nay, wickedness—of those men who do all that is in their power to hinder and hamper boys and girls from the free enjoyment of what alone perhaps constitutes a sufficient justification for the long, unrecorded travail of existence. For let us clear the air of cant and it will be acceded that the hours which on our death-beds we would most care to remember are those fair and happy hours when a fortunate opportunity had been given us to scramble into some honeysuckle thicket with 'Moll, Mag, Marian, or Margery'. There would seem to be a conspiracy amongst us Anglo-Saxons to disparage, as far as is possible, the delights of love-making. That section of society whose chief concern is to perpetuate the stability of their ill-gotten property, take it upon themselves to harness and bridle what is as unstable as quicksilver, as evasive as the light of moonshine. They even endeavour to pervert the natures of their daughters, for the purpose of selling their chastity in the matrimonial market—as though it were contained in an unopened golden casket—to the highest bidder. And what clap-trap issues out of their mouths! All this chat about the evil of sensuality, what is it? Who in God's name has ever known an honest sensualist who has half the evil in his nature that is to be found in these miserable, suppressed, narrow-lipped 'home-guards', who sit perched up at the heads of their family tables between the salt and the pepper, devising sly plans for their own vulgar advancement out of desires that should be left free as the mackerel that in the month of June flick in and out of the sea in Weymouth Bay?

When we reached the Sausalito ferry, it was nearly two o'clock in the morning; and after I had said good-bye to my friend I found that the last boat had gone. I forthwith

retraced my steps up Market Street and took rooms in the
Lincoln Hotel. It was late when I waked the next morning.
However tired I may be, nothing gives me more annoyance
than to find that I have dreamed away the best part of a day.
I am one who prefers to be up with the sun. Like another
Merry Andrew, do not I hear night and day 'Time's Wingèd
Chariot'! Well I comprehend the long occasion I shall have
for unconsciousness, when mouth, nostrils, and ear-holes
are bunged with potter's clay. For this reason I was in an
ill-humour when, after having paid my reckoning, I stepped
out into Market Street, which had assumed already the
everyday commonplace look a town wears at noon when the
last vestige of glamour belonging to the deserted hours of
the early morning has worn off, and the first indications of
the relaxation accompanying the fall of night are as yet un-
observed. I had a mind to breakfast, and breakfast well,
but then I felt unshaven, and eventually decided that the
best thing I could do, in my present mood of discontent,
would be to visit a barber. I entered a small shop and took
my place on a chair opposite an enormous mirror. After the
man had finished, and was removing the moist, hot towels
with which my face had been swathed, I suggested he should
give my hair a good brushing. No sooner, however, did he
touch my head, than the rogue cried out like a yaffle in
spring-time, vehemently asseverating that my scalp was
full of he knew not what filth. At first I was completely
taken aback; but then, remembering how lately I had been
frisking in the glades of the Park, I uttered, with no little
complacence, by way of explanation, the comfortable words

'fir cones'. 'Fir cones be ——' answered my persecutor. 'I'll show you some fir cones.' And with that he went to a drawer and got a comb, and running it through my hair held it up before my eyes, full of the most vile-looking vermin. I was now at my wit's end, and would scarce have known what to do, if the fellow had not offered me a bottle of some preparation which, so he assured me, would kill 'the sons of bastards in no time at all.' The bottle cost five dollars, but I paid the money gladly.

Once back in Sausalito, I gave my head the severest shampoo it had ever had, dousing it the while with the precious concoction. Just as I was completing my toilet my brother John came in. I told him of my trouble. 'You should have taken no notice,' he said. 'When American hairdressers tell me there is something wrong with my hair, I simply say, "I know, I know, I know." ' Like a flash I understood how I had been gulled, understood how this slick skeezicks had by him some hidden supply of hair-lice, which he could draw upon at will, terrifying his more foolish customers into buying his damned bottles of coloured turtle-tincture. And this suspicion was confirmed the next day, when I visited a hair specialist, who entirely reassured me as to the condition of my crown. I confided my adventure to my sweet Nan, as she sat opposite me at a restaurant table, eating a watermelon; and how gaily she laughed, and how prettily, how mischievously, her shameless blue eyes danced! She did not care.

CHAPTER SEVEN

Good Friends

THE FILIPINO servants at the hotel continued to exasperate my brother to such an extent that we were driven to look for quarters elsewhere. Eventually we found what we wanted, and established ourselves in an old-fashioned hostel overlooking the Bay. Our new room was large and possessed seven windows, and because it was light and airy I would often wake at dawn; and on these occasions, in order to pass away the time, I would sometimes take up the newspaper of the day before. One morning, when I was opening this favourite journal of mine, opening it with the particular crackling sound that newspapers make when their great flapping pages are being refolded, my brother John, whom I had imagined fast asleep, suddenly sat bolt up in bed. 'Good Lord!' he exclaimed. 'How the life-energy must come pouring back into you! Think of being able to read a Hearst paper as soon as ever one opens one's eyes! Imagine it! Why, for most of us it takes hours upon hours before we can even contemplate the state of consciousness with any agreeable feeling. I am one,' he went on, 'who believes that arrangements should be made for civilised people to spend the day up to five o'clock with the vegetable world alone, and yet, and yet,' he continued ruefully, 'it is my destiny to sleep in the same room with some one capable of reading the *Examiner*

at six o'clock in the morning.' As soon as he had finished
speaking he put out a long, lean arm (being by now
thoroughly awakened) for a box of Richmond cigarettes,
giving me meanwhile a look full of love and ironic amusement. But how happy I was with him, have always been
with him, with this old Salamander, who is so supersensitive
to the dim consciousness of Nature that on more than one
occasion I have quarrelled with him because I could not
persuade him to sit in a wayside hedge for fear of crushing
the waving grasses which grew there. I know him, who
better? I know how caught in an evil trap he has been, and
how he has been exploited and 'nothing said'. How he has
been compelled by force of circumstances and his own
magnanimity to prostitute his talents and to perform like a
dancing-bear before gatherings made up of people who
understand him not at all. Often and often, with tears in
my eyes, have I watched him set out to give a lecture to a
girls' school, to a women's club, he who by the magic of
his tongue could have made the very ancients exclaim.
Lydia Gibson, whom I met for the first time at Sarah Bard
Field's house, used to declare that I suffered from a 'brother
complex'. Little indeed did she understand! Have not I for
a quarter of a century followed in the wake of John Cowper?
All that I am I owe to him. Like a sagacious Sancho Panza,
I have ever kept close behind his great medieval wain full
of the foison of I know not what rich harvest-field. And
whatever out of its largess his ample wagon gave to the
wayside hedge, that have I had the wit to garner and, with
the panniers of my Dapple well stuffed, to carry shrewdly

off to the nearest market. For let them say what they will, it is John alone of all of us who can be likened to the forked lightning, he alone has undisputed access to those deep, cool wells where the gods themselves let down their buckets.

Of those who have been cognisant of the hidden drama of my brother's life, none has watched it with more sympathy and understanding than has Theodore Dreiser. Many a time have I heard him declare that nothing would please him better than to provide a refuge, a cell, for his friend. The very first time I saw Dreiser, he touched upon this subject. It was at Sausalito; and when he had finished speaking, I remember he turned a heavy quizzical glance on me, as much as to say, 'Well, how is it that you have not a well-balanced pack-saddle on your back, and are not harnessed up with a good stout, breadwinner's breeching?' We were sitting on the verandah of the hotel together, and I read him an essay I had written, entitled *Black Gods*. It did me good to see how the old bully-rook chuckled, as he sat there, rocking himself backwards and forwards, and doing up his handkerchief into a thousand little squares. We saw him off at the Sausalito station; and as we turned the corner, near the patch of grass where I once sat eating a bagful of cherries, I looked round, thereby accidentally impressing upon my mind the visual memory of this ponderous man, with his hands clasped behind his back, striding along the platform, deep in thought. For Theodore Dreiser is one of those who are utterly incapable of swallowing the world as a young cuckoo swallows the grub that its wagtail mother has brought to it. He must look under every leaf, turn over every stone. His great lumbering imagination, full of a divine curiosity, goes roaring through the prairie-lands of the Cosmos with the restless heavy-shouldered force of an old bull *wildebeest*. Whenever I am with him and can watch his cumbersome intellect at work upon any one of the manifold subjects that occupy his attention, subjects like 'the trickiness of women', the breeding of pigeons, the reasoning-power of a spider he studied once in his bed-chamber, or the electronic basis of the Universe, I never fail to be amazed, never fail to feel awe at the struggles of this ungainly giant, whose limbs are still half buried in clay. It was Theodore Dreiser who was with my brother when he had his operation. He put on a white coat and accompanied him into the theatre, talking philosophically with him up to the last moment.

I received the news of Dr. John Erdmann's victory over Death a few days later, in the heart of Africa, as I was crossing a wide sun-scorched plain on my white pony. Indeed, if I visited Kenya again I could without difficulty find my way to the exact spot where the naked negro messenger met me, somewhere between the stunted lilishwa tree and where the baboons used to sit on the escarpment ledges, a little this side of the first water-hole.

It was Theodore Dreiser who wrote a preface for *Ebony and Ivory*. A curious incident happened in connection with this. My publisher told me that it was customary to recompense writers who undertook to sponsor a book, to the tune of fifty dollars. I was astonished by this information; but as I had recently given a lecture at Miss Spence's School,

where I had received a cheque for this very amount, I went
to Dreiser and nervously offered him the hard-earned piece
of paper. He at once concluded that I was handing him a
cheque written out by myself, and seizing it between his
enormous finger and thumb, tore it into a hundred fragments. At that moment I entertained two conflicting
emotions. I felt proud at having come across a man of letters
who so vindicated the high traditions of the profession,
but at the same time I experienced a very real pain in the
region of my wrinkled navel to think of Miss Spence's good
bounty being destroyed in this way. 'The present-day world
is no place for us intellectuals,' Dreiser would remark.
'We are about as much tolerated as a lot of rats who just
manage to secure a livelihood by keeping out of sight.' It
was Theodore Dreiser who had first suggested the publication of *Ebony and Ivory*. He wrote a letter to Mr. Horace
Liveright, who after he had looked over the collection of
essays, went so far as to suggest that he himself should forthwith set about selling each of them separately to the maga-
zines. Half the proceeds of these fortunate transactions were
to go, so he explained, towards the expense of advertising
the book. While I stood bewildered by the flattering plan
of campaign he had presented to my mind, he laid his hand
on my shoulder and graciously told me that I might consider
him as my publisher. Six months later, after an interview
with a sinuous, self-possessed clerk, who made me feel as
I sat opposite him as though I were searching for firm ground
on the Goodwin Sands, I received my manuscript back,
and with it came to me, for the first time, a full apprecia-

tion of the meaning of that 'colourful' and expressive,
American phrase, 'a hot-air artist'. I received very different
treatment at the hands of Otto Liveright, the literary agent,
who, on one occasion, because he knew I was poor, acted
for me and refused to receive a penny for his trouble. While
in America, I continually found myself being accorded the
most surprising and undeserved generosity. Instead of
wishing me to fail, as my brother Theodore has often taught
me to expect, many Americans apparently wished me to
succeed, and would go out of their way, even when they
were strangers, to help me.

John at this time was giving a course of lectures at
Burlingame where the more fashionable Californians live.
I used to accompany him each week to some great house.
There were families who were obviously distinguished,
and others who were not. We visited the richest of all the
houses one afternoon; yet in spite of the display of so much
wealth and so many really beautiful treasures, one wanted
only to run away. We were entertained afterwards by
our hostess, a pretentious woman, who had the waddling
walk of a swan-goose I once saw on the estate of my friend,
Rivers Pollock, in the county of Suffolk. Just as one comes
upon people in America who appear better-bred than any
Europeans, so one occasionally meets men and women who
apparently consider ordinary refinement as quite unnecessary,
so confident are they that their prestige depends entirely
upon their wealth. In New York, I have gone up a marble
staircase behind a liveried servant, to find myself ushered
into the presence of I know not what company. My brother

and I left this particular Californian mansion in amazement at all that we had heard and seen, and were unable to rid our minds of our impression for several hours. The cool green vistas of the colonnade of trees in front of the station could not do it for us, any more than could the look of the stockyards on the outskirts of San Francisco, those stockyards which almost invariably arrested our attention as the train slid past them; with the animals crowded into narrow pens, without food, waiting to be slaughtered for the nourishment of the inhabitants of the brothels of the suppressed Barbary Coast, as well as for the pretty bodies of the incomparably caparisoned ladies whose thoughts had been so lately directed toward the delicate and difficult art of life as understood by Walter Pater and Gabriele d'Annunzio.

It was nearly midnight before we returned to our hotel, advancing step by step along the overgrown paths of the perfumed, moth-haunted summer-garden. The moon was at its full, and my brother insisted upon sitting down at the foot of a great shadowed tree to contemplate the dead planet that has always had so strange an influence over him. And as the light of it, that enchanted white light, flooded down upon us, touching the upper side of every leaf, we felt, as we rested there in that darkened place, something of its divine power. Its radiance was falling, we knew, everywhere, falling upon the jasmine flowers we had seen trailing over the sill of the Burlingame house, falling upon the blunt snouts of the frogs inhaling dew-cool air in pools in the downs, falling on the flat, broad horns of motionless moose, standing in hidden valleys far away in the Rocky Mountains. But as we watched, conscious of the wavering, tremulous mystery of the night as the very insects about us, deep-buried in the long, damp grass, an unwonted thing happened. Suddenly upon the left side of that great luminous disk there appeared a black speck, insignificant as one tiny eye-lash on the cheek of a girl. It enlarged its proportions, invading that silvery surface with a clear hard projection of inky blackness which grew moment by moment greater and greater. Who could describe the ghostly accumulating darkness that fell upon the Sausalito hillside? It was as different from ordinary darkness as the face of a corpse is different from the face of a man asleep. Aha! The equivocal cuckquean! It was the other side of darkness—darkness showing its backside to us, as God showed his to Moses. By accident we had selected the hour of a total eclipse of the moon for our vigil, for watching and praying in that western garden.

> *Treachery in the heavens! From land*
> *And sea and every forest way,*
> *From frightened pastures and darkened sand*
> *Rose up a cry of wild dismay—*

We felt our direction through the dim blackness to the door of the Hollyoak Hotel, and went up into our turreted chamber in silence.

CHAPTER EIGHT

Californian Characters

IT WOULD be hard to deny the beauty of the scenery about San Francisco, or the classical appearance of the city itself, as it rises above its silver bay, tier upon tier. I shall never forget my astonishment when I first arrived in Sausalito and found myself so early in the year, standing knee-deep in grasses and flowers at the door of the hotel; and for weeks the floral spring-time profusion of the downs never failed to startle me, as I came upon it on each folded hillside. At first I liked to see the ubiquitous evergreen oaks matted closely together at the bottom of every combe, and took especial delight in walking beneath the tall, rustling eucalyptus trees, bordering the upland tracks with their hygienic pointed foliage and pink, flaky trunks; but when I learnt that this particular tree was not indigenous to the country, but had been imported from Australia, and that the oak tree of the poet Horace never shed its leaves, I developed an odd antipathy for these purged Western prospects, and, indeed, as the summer drew to a close, became more and more conscious of an insistent nostalgia for the East, for a landscape which each year suffered the privations of a real winter, with forest trees standing naked, their roots covered up in snow. But in spring-time, the clear-eyed cheerfulness of California, cheerful with the conventional cheerfulness of those little flowers which the residents in this novel state feel no shame in calling 'tidy-tips' and 'blue-eyed-babies', has, it cannot be gainsaid, a very definite appeal. It is true that a visitor from the Old World is constantly made uneasy by the feeling that the Americans who populate each modern, up-to-date Californian town are entirely divorced from a countryside suited, perhaps, to Spanish mountain monasteries or Indian wigwams, but certainly in no way adapted to support an invasion of restless, money-making Anglo-Saxons. Yet I lie; for do not I remember, at this very moment, how the ferry-boats each week-end would carry across the bay thousands of boys and girls, 'hikers' (if we are compelled to make use of that hideous word, which, be it noted, we owe to the Filipinos) possessed by an exultation that was purely pagan?

A brave sight it was to see these laborious boats, these happily burdened triremes, let loose on the Sausalito pier their jocund cargoes of pleasure-seekers. And yet, if you can believe it, even during the time I was in San Francisco, there were certain people whose natures were so poisoned by moralic acid that they could, with a free conscience, get up an agitation against allowing these charming excursionists to sleep out in the woods together. Conceive, if you can, the state of mind, the inert malice, latent in men and women who could deliberately set about trying to deprive these children of the only free and happy hours of their working-week. Fortunately, such detestable malt-weevils have ranged against them forces not easy to be overcome. Each summer the great downs lie at the foot of

Mount Tamalpais, like beautiful naked women, and the youth of the city is not slow to take the hint.

However, it would be a mistake, as I have already tried to show, to think that all Californians have the mental outlook of a congress of Methodist ministers. During our stay, my brother and I had the honour of making the acquaintance of Noel Sullivan, a young man, tall and slim and bearded. If ever I want to conjure up for my own satisfaction a type of a perfect aristocrat, I find that my mind immediately reverts to this 'gentleman from San Francisco'. One afternoon he drove us to a country-house belonging to some relation of his. I well recollect the figure he cut, as he stood in the centre of a brilliant green lawn, holding delicately on the end of a long first finger a scarlet macaw; also I remember the expression of religious, sophisticated irony that passed over his ultra-refined countenance, as, stepping out of his motor car, he crossed a grassy lawn, his discreetly polished shoes shining in the late afternoon sun, to peer through the newly cement-set bars of the grille of a convent, built and endowed by his family for the life-long confinement of a score or more young girls, brought here for picturesque imprisonment, as a whim, perhaps, of this young Prince, who, although ashamed of the power his wealth gave him was yet very well able to appreciate the peculiar beauty belonging to any kind of religious ecstasy in a world where all is, at best, so dubious and so fleeting.

Very different from Mr. Sullivan was the redoubtable Dr. Schott. Here, in truth, was an original; I had almost said a genius. In appearance he suggested some alert barber of Piræus, a barber whose head was full of information about the back-lanes of Athens, information that he would impart piecemeal to his customers while he munched raisins from a leather wallet at his side. The fantastic spiral stairways of Dr. Schott's mind were reflected in his fantastical physiognomy, reflected in his pale face and prying nose, and in the protruding flaps of black hair that fell away from the perfect parting in the middle of his head. And, by God, this incomparable jumping-jack knew well enough how to peer through the wainscot cracks of reality! I have been with him when he has set the whole universe agog with his metaphysical whimsies and quaint philosophical tags. Nothing was true, nothing was stable, before the sight of Dr. Schott. That the fellow was as mad as a March magpie I have little doubt. But how quaint and sharp a glance I saw him bestow upon the window in the St. Francis Hotel where Fatty Arbuckle had recently been disporting himself, as he discussed the origin of Christianity and pondered 'what in the devil's name could have started the story going so crazy, crazy!'

I was to see the Doctor on two further occasions before I left America. Once, when he met my friend Kessler, a hard-headed, grave-digging metaphysician, in my rooms in Patchin Place, and once when he returned from some inconceivable excursion on the Continent, carrying in his hands the two lanterns used by the Paris sacristan in burying Anatole France, whose coffin he had actually seen being tossed in the air by a crew of frisky Gauls, who had undertaken to carry the body of their good, atheistical, catholic master to its grave.

The meeting in Patchin Place was especially amusing to me. Here were juxtaposed two of the most eccentric philosophers that it has ever been my privilege to meet. Often and often had I been depressed by my logger-headed friend Kessler bringing out, by way of an introduction to some abstruse discourse, that stale, flat, and unprofitable line of argument which begins by asserting that nothing in itself exists; but when, upon this occasion, the old curmudgeon, sensing that the Doctor was philosophically inclined, began to talk in the same strain, pointing out that the water-jug on the table had an existence only in our minds, you might have thought that the Devil had jumped into the room, by the clamour that arose. 'Good God!' yelled the Doctor, raising his crested poll like any farmyard chanticleer in Æsop's fables who is reasoning with the town bull, 'don't try to put that cock over on me!'

Kessler in many ways was an interesting man. He arrived suddenly in my rooms in Patchin Place, having drifted across the continent from San Francisco, in order to return a book he had borrowed from my brother. He got work as a grave-digger in a Jewish cemetery. It used to tickle my heart to think of this tough-minded friend of mine 'tucking in', day after day, the corpses of New York Jews. I could imagine him so well, standing aside, shovel in hand, this believer in annihilation, while the professional mourners, 'soothsayers' he used to call them, played their part. I could so well envisage the expression of silent, snorting scorn that his countenance would manifest as he waited 'to get on with his day's work'. There was something free and hard about him that one could only admire; and the eyes that looked out from under his dark forehead were always dog-like and firm. I used to enjoy listening to the stories he told of his adventures: how once, far away in the West, he had slept on a heap of green wheat, and how he had been waked in the morning by the dainty triangular feet of partridges stepping about over him, and how he had got up and gone to a near-by spring and dipped a crust of dry bread in its cold waters, so that he might partake of the blessed sacrament of a down-and-out, of a tramp and a rover, who felt at that moment more happy than he has ever felt since in his life.

CHAPTER NINE

Found Wanting

ALTHOUGH SAN FRANCISCO had many diverting forms of amusement to offer to an easy-going traveller, yet it will always remain a grief to me that the Barbary Coast had already been closed down before I visited the city. Long afterwards, as I sat over a chestnut-wood fire in an old Colonial farmhouse far up in the Catskill Mountains, with the snow like a little ermine mat drifting in under the door, I listened, with absorbed interest, to Walter Franzen's descriptions of what it had been like; how it had resembled one of those enthralling pictures of the Broad Road to Destruction, such as our old cook, the daughter of Charles Childs, the Montacute clerk, used to hang up in her bedroom. Sitting there, over a crackling fire, with our tomcat, Tipoo, perched on the old four-poster bedstead, watching in an attitude of feline craft its own pointed shadow on the wall, I had the scene brought vividly before my eyes—the noisy street lit by a hundred lights, the Salvation Army girls snatching at the sleeves of the young men, imploring them to remember their mothers; and the long rows of houses, fitted with swinging-doors through which one passed, to select at will any of the inmates, who, like painted artificial flowers, lovely to look upon, kept calling out to each newcomer the intimate secrets of their art. Returning late at night from Colonel

Wood's house on Russian Hill, I used often to pass through this quarter of the town, but I never saw anything to excite my attention; indeed, at such times, my chief preoccupation used to be lest some bandit should spring out at me from behind a piled-up heap of 'Sunkist' orange boxes, for it was always my pleasure to pass through the deserted fruit-market, the smell which rose from the great store of fruit and vegetables garnered there being particularly grateful to my nostrils.

Once on the ferry-boat, I would sit looking out at the lights of the terraced city, at the lights on the Island prison, until, with a heavy jolt and a sound of gurgling water, the huge flat-bottomed barge would drift into position between the tall, creaking pier-posts, which, one could see, as the electric light shone upon them, were streaked with the white excrement of sea-gulls. For the bay was crowded with sea-gulls, herring-gulls, like those I used to watch crossing New York City in the early dawn, like those which had been familiar to me from childhood along the white chalk-cliffs of Dorset. I suppose it is more than probable that if some stellar being were to come out of far space to visit the earth, these birds, glancing in the clear morning air, would be among the first sights to reassure such a one that there was life upon this grass-grown sea-glimmering planet.

I used to enjoy looking over the bay at night. I remember, at the end of an evening I spent with Frederick O'Brien, being reminded by a word, a gesture, how inexhaustible was the romance of this harbour, which forms so dramatic a link between West and East. 'Sir Francis Drake,' so he told me, 'had missed it, probably because of a fog, as he sailed up the coast on his famous voyage round the world.' And as I stood there on the small balcony of his house, I took a hint from this Irishman, who was so completely natural, so completely devoid of any form of conceit, and yet whose sense of adventure was so vivid that he had been able, by the power of his pen, to stimulate the imaginations of half the reading public of America.

I would sometimes leave the hotel for a day's excursion. I remember I went up to the top of Mount Tamalpais, sitting in an open-air carriage of the small railway, with my eyes, as we slid upwards, intimately observing each patch of scrub on the near bank, while a fellow with an official's braided cap kept bawling through a megaphone apposite commentaries upon the landscape we passed, in the hope, perhaps, of diverting our minds from the very real apprehension (felt by me, at any rate) lest the absurd conveyance in which we were travelling should suddenly start zigzagging backwards and hurl us to perdition amongst the redwood trees in the valley below. For some obscure reason I always harboured a prejudice against redwood trees. Was it, perhaps, that their appeal to the imagination is so obvious a one, an appeal capable of being appreciated altogether too easily by the kind of middle-aged gentlemen who, under a portrait of Robert Louis Stevenson, concentrated their cultured intellects upon profitable speculations in the commercial world? It cannot be denied, however, that actually to touch the bark of a tree whose trunk, beyond all possible dispute, has felt upon its russet crevices the light of the sun which rose over California on the morning after the crucifixion is an experience most particular. And yet the mere realisation of so unnatural a circumstance necessitates too mean a jump for one's mind, and disposes one to resent such inordinate longevity in the vegetable world, just as one resents being told by a circus-master, in evening dress and top-hat, that a certain elephant was born in the reign of Queen Elizabeth. In the face of such stubborn anachronisms, expatiated upon at length by a gold-braided guide, one almost finds it in one's heart to wish that the earth would open wide and swallow up such antiquated timber. I understand that Californians do get shaken about once in a while, but I fear it must require more than any ordinary jolt to disturb the profound equanimity of the frequenters of the Bohemian Club! Just as a night spent in a hurricane at the top of a redwood tree failed to inject any real wisdom into the hard Scotch head of John Muir, seeing that it requires much more than half-a-dozen fir cones in one's beard before one is able to see visions on the road to Damascus.

My brother never cared for such expeditions; so that, when he was with me, we would content ourselves with walking up the high lanes leading to the downs behind the village, often enough returning in a cold, drifting mist, to take tea in a little shop down by the water, where a round-faced Serb, standing behind a counter, would fill a brown-china teapot, acquired by us with the greatest difficulty, with water boiled in a saucepan. I myself would often bespeak a fresh fish or a half-dozen smelts, for I liked to see them sizzling on the honest fellow's great gridiron, a gridiron designed after the exact pattern of the one he had used as a sea-cook. In truth, this Serb on the waterfront of Sausalito was extraordinarily wise and extraordinarily philosophic; and when he was handing one a plate of potatoes, done to a turn, with his sleeves rolled up and his powerful forearm exposed, one could almost believe that if every one had a little geniality and the capacity for working efficiently at their own jobs, most of the world's problems would be solved. It turned out, however, that even the Serb lacked sufficient sagacity; for, happening one day to step out into the road in order to obtain a better view of a schooner, he was knocked over by a passing automobile and thrown, like the globose pod of a broad bean, clear across the way, and almost into that very sea out of which came the fish he knew so well how to serve up sprinkled all over with toasted breadcrumbs.

Until this evil chance overtook him I used to feel nothing but shame at watching him deal so deftly with his orders, each pan when out of use being immediately hung up on its dedicated nail. How wonderful, I thought, to be able to make oneself useful at this rate, to be able to take so efficient a part in the world's work! It appeared that I myself had been born out of due time. If I was not content to be a scurvy schoolmaster, I could imagine no possible niche in the body politic I could fill. As for my writing, it seemed to have come to nothing. No article or essay that I sent East was ever accepted. The mere fact of heading my letter with the word California seemed sufficient to ensure the rejection of the manuscript, the editors concluding out of hand that I was just another weak amateur of letters, such as dwell in their thousands amid the orange-groves of Santa Barbara and Los Angeles. As a life of dependent security seemed still distasteful to me, I determined that as soon as my money was spent I would get back to New York City and starve myself into success. '*Examiner! Examiner!*' I would hear the newspaper-sellers outside the San Francisco station cry; and their raucous utterance, so ephemeral and so inconsequent, would go quivering past the soda-water fountains, go quivering past the store of the man who sold little purple figs, out and on and up, to where the station-tower projected its modern post-earthquake embattlements into a midnight metallic sky. And as I listened to their shrill, strangled reiteration of the disturbing word, and was even accosted by the poor derelict half-wits who were shouting it out, derelict half-wits who had been driven into the open like a lot of frantic whistling mice, I would say to John, 'That's what I ought to be doing,' and he would for answer give me a look full of indulgent amusement, making as though he wished to dig his chin into me, and a moment later be stooping to pick up a piece of asparagus-grass, the most artificial and contemptible grass that exists, lest the identity with which it had been endowed by the brain of a madman, its dubious scrap of consciousness, receive further humiliation under the rubber O'Sullivan heels of 'commuters', who, to the tune of a cent-in-the-slot Victrola, were hurrying forward, in complete unconcern, over the marble floors patched with chewing-gum in every possible gradation of being stamped flat.

CHAPTER TEN

New York Again

WE LEFT for the East some time in the beginning of October. How magnetic is the appeal of New York at this season of the year, when, like rooks returning to their king rookery, everybody comes crowding into the great city, into this perpendicular modern Babylon, with its proud, hard, dogtooth outlines! I have often walked down Fifth Avenue with a feeling of antipathy for what has met my eyes, with a feeling of antipathy for the sharp, pretty women, so extravagantly dressed in furs that I knew had been flayed from the frozen backs of a thousand little wood-creatures; with a feeling of antipathy for the shop-windows, with their display of expensive frippery; with a feeling of antipathy for the polished automobiles at the curb, with their obsequious attendants; but never have I experienced any emotions of this kind in the fall. Then, at the time of the first white frosts, when the homely New England countryside is fragrant with the sweet scent of little withered grapes, I could never find it in my heart to curse this town, which, like some vast battery, is capable of recharging with eager electricity the most inert brains, the most weary thighs and ankles. God, how I have seen the Flatiron Building stand out against an afternoon sky in November, stark and naked! With what glee coursing through my live bones have

I not approached Eighth Street, the air just tainted with
the fresh cold of winter, to observe Mr. Robert Parker,
that heavy-headed, glaucous-eyed Pyrrho of the studios,
full of fantastic spites and cloudy disparagements, hovering
as if suspicious of the veracity of the very compass points
of the city, to catch sight a moment later, of the familiar
faces of the Brevoort barbers peering out of their underground door like so many Guy de Maupassants; and to be
diverted at every turn by fresh Greenwich Village types,
fantastical men with charming girls at their elbows, girls
with free eyes and bodies that looked dedicated to the sole
purpose of giving delight to artists in a hundred little hidden-
away upstair studios. To sneer at Greenwich Village has
always to me seemed unfair. In a world where the lives
of most of us are so unspeakably drab, it offers many a green-
hooded snake a very real refuge. I doubt but it would be
found that the most civilised people in America live within
a bowshot of Jefferson Market. If the young men and maidens
are a trifle extravagant, so much the better. Their eccen-
tricities have the effect of frightening away unpleasant people,
so that honest writers may live as they like, unmolested by
the hideous social tyrannies of a barbarous commercial
age.

The first night of our arrival we put up at the Seville
Hotel. After I had signed my name in the register, the clerk
said: 'Are you the Llewelyn Powys who writes about
Africa?' I took these words as a good omen, and retreated
toward the elevator, trying to pass off as lightly as I might
that most pleasant sensation of finding one's identity has

made some kind of impression upon the great alien outside world.

We slept in the same room; but because of my presence, my brother did not have a good night. 'Merely to feel that there is another brain shut up in the same room with me is sufficient to interfere with my sense of complete peace. What I love is a sense of oblivion, nothingness,' he said. The next morning we went looking for rooms, and eventually found one in Waverly Place, an 'enormous room', lit up on fine afternoons by the reflection of the sun from factory windows opposite. So ill-furnished was it, and so incapable were we of making it at all comfortable, that on fine mornings I used to do most of my writing in Washington Square, though even this plan was not always successful, because of the little bootblack boys, who, every two or three minutes, would come round importunately shouting, 'Shine! Shine! Shine!'

When my brother was away, I used to fill up my afternoons and evenings with engagements; and now that I had become so poor, I was apprehensive lest my polite clothes might be stolen from me and even this means of escape be closed down. Arnold Shaw, my brother's frolicsome manager, had, so it happened, that very summer, preserved his apartment intact from burglary by the use of a police-lock which had proved altogether too much for the jemmies of the bandits. When he came to see me, he urged me strongly to invest in one of these clever devices. 'Burglars,' he said, as he looked casually out of the blank, screenless windows, 'probably, I should think, run through

the houses of this street on an average of about once a month.'
Immediately my mind reverted to a magnificent overcoat
I possessed, and already I began to experience a premonition
of the misery I would suffer if it was taken from me. So it
came to pass that my brother found himself the inhabitant
of a room bare as a barn, and yet protected like a prison,
with the most ingenious contrivance ever invented by man's
brain. For, whenever he went out of the room, even so
much as to wash his hands in the bathroom, an iron rod
that was craftily inserted into the floor would, with an ugly
clank, slip automatically into its place in the lock, rendering
by this means our disagreeable garret, with its coal-bag
and heap of splintered kindling, absolutely impregnable
until I, from the inside, had executed certain delicate manipu-
lations.

Never shall I forget the look of amazed wonder on the
face of my friend Jack Kelly, when he dropped in to ask
me to tea one day and found my door in full working order.
Jack Kelly was a picturesque figure. Nothing used to please
me better than to see him come striding round some corner
with a devilish Irish thorn in his hand, and his magnificent
chest covered with a brave corduroy waistcoat. And how
the old bully used to enjoy his dinners at Broad's, eating
great tenderloin steaks ('of the dun ox, you know') at his
favourite table, with his matchless Anne Valentine at his
side, sensitive and perceptive, listening to him discoursing
to his friends on how he and she and one other sailed his
yacht at large over the Atlantic and were entertained by
the world of fashion at Cowes! Jack Kelly was, indeed, as

fine a brave as I have ever seen, and not the kind of man that one would select by choice to cuckold. One day, as I was having my shoes polished on a raised chair outside Frank Shay's bookshop, I suddenly noticed Jack Kelly, standing motionless in the middle of the street, with his eyes apparently concentrated upon the roof of Jefferson Market, where, I took it, must be a boy's kite, or a pigeon, or two amorous roof-cats at play. I called out asking him what it might be that had caught his attention. He replied that he was studying the weather signs, having a mind to set sail that very afternoon to God only knew what distant port.

In spite, however, of the barrenness of our dwelling-place (the old black-and-tan terrier, Nip, in our father's mansion being housed better than we), there were moments in the day when we were happy; especially when, after breakfast, after our coffee and rolls at the French pastry shop, we took a turn round Washington Square, full of talk about this or that. John would look with entertainment at the statue of Garibaldi, with its baggy trousers, and sword forever half drawn from its sheath, a veritable symbol of the feeble ineffectiveness of popular discontent, and with undisguised surprise at the countenance of Mr. Holly, the inventor—or discoverer, was it?—of Bessemer steel. 'Good Lord,' he once declared, 'what a shame to have such an image here! Why the site is magnificent! They ought to commission the most extravagant of all the artists in the Village to carve a monument to Priapus on this spot, a monument which, like the statue of Memnon, would utter a cry each morning, as soon as the sun spread its rays down Washington Place.' We used to like to wander under the English elms and look up through their naked branches, covered with the crinkled bark that was so dear to our eyes. In the same mood, in the springtime, we would go from our rooms, to inspect the slow growth of a certain dock, which one day we had noticed coming up near the railings of the Benedict. We both of us felt strangely restored by daily observing the broad leaves of this simple plant widen and widen, those same leaves that had cured our nettle stings as children, and that had been used by the yeoman in the *Canterbury Tales* for keeping away from his sweating forehead the hot yellow sunshine of the Kentish highroad.

What would disconcert us more than anything, on our return to our room to make my brother's bed, was the fact that the dust on the bare floor seemed in our absence to have been mysteriously and spontaneously generated into funny fluffy balls that had the shape and appearance of curled-up, hibernating, grey mice, and yet were light enough to roll over and over at the slightest flap of the sheet. There was only one bed to make, as I was sleeping on the roof, sleeping without a mattress, but wrapped well round with blankets and two red baize curtains, which had at one time belonged to the 'end room' at Montacute Vicarage.

CHAPTER ELEVEN

Hall-Bedrooms

IN THE early part of December my brother once more left for the West, and it became clear to me that if I was to support myself by my pen I would have to find a cheaper room than the spacious fortified barrack in which we had been living. If I could hire a hall-bedroom for ten or twelve dollars a month, I would be able, I thought, to get on all right. For several mornings I searched in the poorer streets toward the river. It was a peculiarly depressing occupation. Dressed in my old African red shirt, and a pair of khaki trousers, I mounted scores of stone steps, steps worn and chipped, to pull at scores of broken bell-handles, in order to interview scores of bedraggled landladies. I had no conception that such people were still living. It was amazing. One after another they stood before me, decrepit human alley-cats, with knots of grey unbrushed hair falling upon their soiled blouses, like the elf-locks one sees in the manes of aged mares that are past work, and yet retain a sufficient fund of energy to display certain vicious characteristics developed by them through long years of ill-usage. Quite apart from the degrading effect of penury, I think that the profession of renting rooms has a most evil influence on human beings. To make one's living out of providing so simple a necessity as a rain-proof roof must bring into play a kind of atavistic meanness, the meanness of a taloned female who has secured a good cleft in the rock or a good forked branch. How sordid and squalid were the rooms into which I was conducted, rooms that smelt of gas, rooms that gave out the faint, chill aroma of damp, fly-blown wall-paper, rooms that affected one's spirits with the lugubrious, concentrated weight of all the forgotten rainy afternoons that had ever fallen upon New York City! Some of these old women would eye me with a kind of salacious avarice, others with an unmoved, bloodshot glare, as if they were already making exact calculations as to the number of soiled dollar-notes that my depravity and despair were likely to bring to their tattered purses before I fell to even lower levels of life. With nervous tread I would tiptoe over the frayed oilcloth carpets to look out of the window, carpets that had, perhaps, been lying in the same place through the bitter Januaries and the humid Augusts of sixty New York seasons, carpets worn bare to the boards below by the muddy, uneven boot-heels of numberless single-room bachelors. And to look out of these small back windows with one of these hostile women at my side, women whose indrawn personalities were as powerful as the clinging, adhesive tentacles of a defiled fish, on to the backs of houses with washtubs suspended from the nails by each window, on to desolate roofs and walls stained with filth and grime, was to receive a revelation as to the pernicious power that a foul human environment might have upon the mind. With a feeling of infinite nostalgia I remembered how once I had ridden over wide African plains, where the hoofs of my stallion had clicked against the bones of lions; where there had been places so removed from mankind and the traps they lay for one another, that a sow rhinoceros could suckle her young, completely ignorant that there existed in the world an erect anthropoid as unprecedented in its cunning and ferocity as *homo sapiens*.

I had often noticed a hotel on Sixth Avenue which advertised rooms at twenty-five cents a night, and it seemed to me that I might perhaps persuade the landlord of it to rent me one of these on a more permanent basis. After all, I thought, if I could have a small room where my clothes would be safe, and where I could do my typewriting, I would be happy enough. I turned into the place and climbed up a long flight of stairs, which led into a large waiting-room, where some twenty men were engaged in reading newspapers. The landlord approached me and I told him what I wanted. He was a competent fellow, with the disposition of a master of a workhouse, at once stern and kindly, but I was unable to interest him in my affairs. 'This place would not do for you,' he kept repeating. Eventually I persuaded him to show me the twenty-five cent rooms. They were cubicles opening on to a narrow central passage, which was dark as night. My guide urged me in a whisper to walk as quietly as possible along this grim catacomb, lest I should wake the sleepers on each side of me. I left the house, descending once more the wide staircase, each step of which was tipped with iron, never to enter it again. I used to look at it often enough, though, as I waited for the down-town elevated train at Eighth Street, craning my neck, like a speckled starling on a roof-top, to get a better view of the waiting room, which remained always full of men reading crumpled newspapers, with apparently no gaps in their ranks. And, as I looked at that melancholy, dispirited interior, I would think of those others, further within, who like rats in the darkened, dolorous holes, were enjoying for '25 cents' a blessed respite from the heartless, ferret-like ferocity prevailing on the other side of the swinging-door encased in triple brass, of this retreat 'for bachelors only'.

As a matter of fact, all my trouble had been wasted; for when I announced to my landlady that I intended to leave, she suggested that I occupy a small room on the same landing as the staircase which led to the roof, a bedroom which I found in every way suitable, and where I was to live for the next few months. Charles Divine, the poet and short story writer, inhabited the floor below me, and I would often consult him as to the secrets of the trade we followed, and envy him his mastery of a technique which still seemed to me extremely intricate and extremely difficult. For in spite of all my efforts I remained very poor. I would spend hour after hour studying a little paper called 'How to Write!' With envy in my heart I would read the autobiographical accounts of how this or that author became successful, became the master of so many thousand of dollars a year, in no time at all. I would study this remarkable publication in a cheap restaurant frequented by draymen, a restaurant which presented a plate-glass front to two separate streets. There we would sit like queer fish in an illuminated aquarium, for all men's eyes to see. Now and again we would get up and leave our places and go to the counter to have our cups of thick white china filled with coffee at five cents a cup. And it would be so cold often outside, with the snow fluttering down on the pavement, that one could not fail to be grateful for the warmth of the place, for the warm atmosphere that enveloped one as soon as one pushed the door open, an atmosphere smelling of dirty sawdust, tobacco, and stale human sweat. Sometimes I would have my lunch as well as my breakfast in this establishment, but I never did so without regretting it afterwards. The food was more fit for the debased appetite of famished hyenas than for human beings; and one could not help wondering how long ago it must have been since the day when the grass-eaters, at whose greasy bones we gnawed, had been driven in from their pastures for the last time. There I would sit, with my elbows resting on the table of sham marble, reading my absurd magazine and filling my coffee with more and more sugar, dipped out of a bowl with a spoon coated over with grains of sweetness congealed by the coffee of earlier guests; and as I sipped the brown syrup I would look at a heap of unripe grapefruit, whose pale lemon-coloured skins, more than anything else, seemed to suggest the bitter meagreness of the provender upon which at this period of my life it had pleased the good God that I should live. But my moods of depression would never last long. I would soon find my spirits rising. Could I not, if the worst came to the worst, go up-town to one of the houses of the great, where at least I should be able to smoke a good cigarette? For in these days I gave up smoking entirely.

It was the *Freeman* that really kept me afloat. For some reason or other my style of writing hit the fancy of Mr. Nock. My paper on Nicholas Culpeper, which had gone to every magazine in the city, won from him the greatest commendation, and was followed by several other literary appreciations of old-fashioned, out-of-the-way English writers. Meanwhile, Mr. Van Wyck Brooks began to feel more confidence in my power as a reviewer. I used to enjoy going to the *Freeman*. The atmosphere of the office seemed to reflect the benevolent rulings of its master. As one mounted the staircase, one was as likely as not to catch a glimpse of the Editor of the *Freeman* expatiating to three or four trig maidens on some abstruse point which presumably had to do with single tax. One would see this interior vignette and hurry on, carrying in one's mind, however, the engaging picture of a grey-haired, elderly gentleman, who looked like the sporting publican of Glanville Wotton just home from the Blackmore Vale Point to Point races, entertaining three very pretty ladies, who, in the most graceful postures imaginable, were perched on the edge of the table. Indeed, the charming picture would remain in one's mind even while Van Wyck Brooks, with nervous, reserved affability, was shaking one's hand as a preliminary to looking over his shelves, as one stood at the door in extreme embarrassment, trying to preserve one's balance, in a silence that each moment was growing more and more audible. Mr. Walter Fuller used at that time to be associated with the journal, and I would often go direct to the room of this Dorset man, in whose company I felt, naturally enough, completely at my ease. Mr. Walter Fuller had a heart of pure gold. In any New York office other than the *Freeman* he would have appeared out of place. He possessed the kind of goodness that it is difficult for an American business man to appreciate, the goodness of a clod of earth out of which a plant of clover is growing, the goodness of a basket of last year's pippins, the goodness of a soft-crusted cottage-loaf baked in a village oven. As one talked to him and heard him declaim against the crude noises of Macdougal Street, or the latest iniquity that had been perpetrated by some unscrupulous money-magnate, one realised in a moment how impossible it was for him to learn to dance to the American tune, and this in spite of the fact that he had won for his partner so splendid, so triumphant an amazon as Crystal Eastman. As he stood fumbling with the papers on his desk, he would remind me of a barn-door owl who had been betrayed into forsaking the ivy-mantled tower of Sturminster Newton, and, having crossed the Atlantic with soft, downy flight, finds itself on the top of an iron-ribbed skyscraper, surrounded by flocks of over-sized American robins infuriated at the presence of so homely an apparition. A very different type was Francis Neilson, whom I ran into one day on the second landing. He had been a Liberal member of Parliament and had all the good-natured, hearty bluster of a person of that kind. Yet in spite of the fact that he selected of his own free will to stay in a hotel like the Ritz-Carlton, there was something extremely honest about the man. I certainly felt this on the occasions when, having made my way through swarms of loud, overdressed people on the palatial ground floor of his favourite residence, and having mounted the elevator manipulated by a pale flunkey, and having walked down a corridor on a silent puffed-up carpet, I found myself at last eating hot toast and listening to the exuberant, semi-philosophic observations of this rich man, who, although hardly prepared to sell all he had to give to the poor, yet could not be dissuaded, within certain well-defined limits, from doing whatever was in his power to prevent oppression and foster the cause of freedom.

At this time, also, I received encouragement from sources other than the *Freeman*. One morning, as I was returning from my bath to my small upstairs room, carrying my sponge, soap, towel, and the key to unlock my door (for I had not yet overcome my dread lest some sneak-thief should snatch up my superb greatcoat), my tooth-glass slipped from its position in the crook of my elbow, and, glancing on to the banister, fell with a crash to the floor below. Fearing lest some fellow lodger might cut his feet on the broken glass, I went downstairs again to pick up as many pieces as I could see. I had hardly been on my knees a minute, when a door opened, and a young man, a perfect stranger to me, came out on the landing. There was something so intellectual about his face, something so candid and disarming, that I stayed talking with him for several minutes. He asked me what I did and I told him that I made a living by writing about Africa. He then remarked that only that week he had bought six copies of the *North American Review* because it contained an essay called 'A Leopard by Lake Elmenteita', by a man named Llewelyn Powys, which he considered a rare example of true, living prose in the best English tradition. And as I knelt there on that dusty carpet, picking up tiny fragments of splintered crystal, just as a pigeon might pick up grains of rice, I felt a glow of elation at hearing such praise on my work from this stranger with a great cerebral moon-face and the handshake of a farmer. I should have felt even more elation had I known how greatly I would come to respect in later days the literary judgments of my friend Paul Piel, inventor, sculptor, philosopher.

CHAPTER TWELVE

Patchin Place

A LITTLE BEFORE my brother had left, a mysterious letter had arrived for me from some one in Patchin Place, with an invitation for tea on a certain afternoon. The handwriting was spiderlike and intellectual, and reminded me of Oscar Wilde's handwriting as I remember it in his letters to Louis Wilkinson. I wrote, accepting the invitation, and, with that humiliating inability to foresee the future from which all mortal men suffer, tossed the note over to John to ask him whether it was the script of a man or woman. No suspicion, no inkling, did I have that the white page that fluttered from the table to the bare, dusty floor was the first token of a relationship that was to have so much significance in my life.

On the appointed afternoon I found my way to the famous alley, and was presently enchanted to discover myself sitting down to tea before a bright fire in a lamp-lit room filled with delightful old-fashioned furniture. These rooms suggested to my mind my rooms in the Old Court of Corpus, and were entirely different from anything I had seen elsewhere in New York, as, indeed, was the poise, the intellectual intensity, the freedom from preconceptions, as of a child uncontaminated by the world, of my grave, delicately ironic hostess, whose round, white arms seemed to me then, as I looked at them in the flickering light of the cannel-coal fire, as delectable as dairy junket, and whose fair hair, worn so as to conceal as far as possible the prominence of an over-high forehead, was of a fairer and more fine texture than ever was the hair of that lovely chatelaine who so long ago would sit beneath the glittering holly trees of Brittany, watching her madcap children playing in the coarse seaside grass. And as the weeks and months followed one another, I fell more and more under the influence of the sweet security of Patchin Place, until all my other familiar haunts seemed, one by one, to grow dull—until, indeed, I felt no contentment of spirit unless I knew that I was on that very day to find myself knocking on the darkened door of this particular sanctuary of civilisation. And as the fortunate acquaintance grew, and I became more and more privileged, the reluctance I felt at going back to sleep 'on the roof' steadily increased, until, at length, it came to such a pass that I would rather have 'gone copsing' than have returned to Waverly Place, and, in truth, could not be persuaded to do so on nights when it rained or snowed. For on those dark January nights, when a freezing snow was falling, when but to think of the streets was to remember horses one had seen in the afternoon struggling helplessly on the ground, proud horses who would never again eat hay in darkened subterranean stables, but were probably even now being carried away to the knackers, with hairy, frozen hocks protruding out of a lorry, the small room of my lady's home would appear to me the safest, the snuggest retreat in the world. With its iron grate filled with live coals that from Michaelmas to All Fools' Day were never allowed to go out,

and which toward midnight would glow with a most divine
glow, the little chamber, whose single window, heavily
protected with winter curtains, looked out upon a sheltered
back-yard, reminded me of a room in a fisherman's cottage
on the edge of the Chesil beach at Portland, into which I
had once stepped, a lost traveller coming in out of the
darkness, out of the turbulent winds and drifting salt spray,
to see a woman sewing at a table and an old man mending
tarred fishing nets before just such a fire of sea-coal. As
behind the whitened stone walls of that simple habitation
human beings could be secure, could hear each other speak,
could thread needles, and turn down the lamp when it
smoked, though outside, within fifty yards of them,
enormous uplifted Atlantic waves broke themselves with
a deafening roar and an appalling resurgent eddy upon a
gigantic barrier of pebbles, so in this tiny bed chamber one
could feel at peace and out of harm's way, while, hour after
hour, the lighted city with its frozen heart trembled and
contracted and awaited the coming of dawn.

In those days, as I slipped out in the early hours of the
morning, like a fox from a poultry-yard of delectable White
Wyandottes, I used to regard the caretaker of the alley with
the utmost trepidation, looking back at her with a slanting
apprehensive eye as she poked about with her besom
between the iron railings which protected each small cat-
soured garden lying between pavement and house. She was
a German woman, who had lived in Patchin Place for forty
years, had lived there amongst her ash-cans and the leaves
of the Ailanthus trees—leaves that in April open out like

the webbed feet of goslings—since the day when at Dorchester, in the county of Dorset, John remembered seeing
the skin at the top of my head fluttering up and down,
because, forsooth, the bone in my infant's skull had not
closed up. She was very stout, so stout, in fact that her two
legs had been hard put to it to support so great a weight,
and had developed varicose veins, which necessitated her
winding vast bandages about them. During the summer
months it was her custom to sit all day long at her open
window, her breasts resting on the sill like a pair of enormous
pumpkins. Common people would laugh at her behind her
back and call her 'The Venus'.

Certainly from the way she used to watch the ash-cans at
the corner and abuse the tenants if they mixed their cinders
and garbage, one would have thought that the chief concern
of her mind was with sordid matters. Nothing was further
from the truth. Somewhere concealed within those moun-
tainous rolls of flesh there existed a spirit refined and
romantic. I used often in later days to sit in the old woman's
room and get her to tell me stories about Germany, stories
which had for me the beauty of certain simple country
objects, like the weathered boards from the wing of a windmill, or the worn curving handle of an old scythe. She spoke
broken English, and I would sit opposite her on a rocking-
chair, enthralled by the stammering speech of this peasant
woman, who, with the most uncouth phraseology, was able
to bring so vividly before my eyes certain experiences of her
childhood. For her mind always reverted to Germany,
always reverted to that extraordinary Northern land, in-

habitated by a people whose natures are capable only of the profound feeling of so many milch-cows who go up and down their pastures lowing for their lost calves. But as I rested in her little room, indolently watching through the window the movements of an old tomcat, victor of a hundred battles, with but the shreds of ears left on his flat head, she would tell me of her home, and how once, as a little girl, she had walked all day through the Black Forest to fetch some flax which her neighbours had told her was of a better quality than the flax with which she and her mother were accustomed to spin, and how, in the late afternoon, coming into a dell, with the sun slanting through the leaves 'like faëry land', she had suddenly seen a group of stags 'with golden branches on their heads'. So direct, so poetical, was her talk, that I carried away with me certain glimpses of Germany as ₁clear in my mind as old prints, so that later I would almost feel as if I, even I, had been at the side of the young awkward Gretchen, as she made her way along those meandering woodcutter-tracks that penetrated so far into the great medieval forest, and are still frequented, even in our day, by animals as delicately designed as unicorns 'with golden branches on their heads'.

Poor old 'Mother Wiedeswaller', she never saw Germany again; for just as she was preparing to go home, and had made inquiries about her ticket, she was taken violently ill, and was carried away to Bellevue Hospital. I went to see her there. She was lying on her side, and reminded me of a hippopotamus I once saw supporting its vast wounded bulk on its forelegs, unable, in spite of all its efforts, to re-enter the water of the near-by lake. She recognised me at once. 'Misser Powys,' she said, 'I come back next week.'

I was glad enough to escape from the melancholy room, where each pale head, upon each pale sheet, seemed to represent a final disaster, no longer now to be concealed or evaded. How I hated the competent nurse at the door, trained to display no kind of emotion in the face of all these pitiful dramas! How I shrank from the busy attendants whom I met in the corridors outside, pushing horribly light-wheeled cots, containing bandaged figures, already too weak to protest, to I knew not what hygienic rooms of surgical efficiency; and how, as I at last got into the street and was passing the 'flower shop', I chuckled to myself to see two young doctors in white coats beck and nod at a pair of stenographers, who, with the light step of holiday girls on the Weymouth esplanade, were advancing along the opposite pavement! Yes, as I walked away from that Bastille of Sorrow, it gave me brave consolation to realise that nothing, not death, nor disease, nor piercing agony, is capable of cowing, of shaming into quiescence, that incorrigible heathen force that we call life, and which is as quick to jump, and as inimical to cessation as a little red flea on a nipping frosty morning. As I had already surmised, 'Mother Wiedeswaller' was not speaking correctly when she said, 'Misser Powys, I come back next week'; for by the following Thursday, instead of being back in her room, sitting over her stove, in which in her thrifty German way, she had for two score years burnt her garbage, a proceeding from which she derived every day a peculiar satisfaction, seeing that it meant that refuse itself was made to contribute to her comfort, she was lying in state in an undertaker's parlour—a monumental paragon of cleverly disguised corruption—somewhere at the lower end of Christopher Street. The money which she had saved, and which she had kept so carefully in aprons and stockings, was sent to her relations in Germany, to the extreme annoyance of her immediate neighbours. 'The party what done everythink, he gets nothink,' said an old man to me, who, in spite of a congenital dislike of any form of physical activity other than the relighting of the stump-end of a cheap cigar, had, upon occasions, been persuaded by the old lady to perform certain odd jobs for her in the alley.

CHAPTER THIRTEEN

Excursions

NOTHING AT this time used to give me more satisfaction than to go for excursions out of New York with my chosen companion. If we had only a few hours allotted us, we would take the steamer to the Statue of Liberty, and, following round the little island, would eventually come to a certain strip of deserted sand, where we could sit in the sun, with the forked ridge of the city rising out of the grey waters in happy perspective. It used to delight us to find shells and small scraps of water-moulded glass and even pieces of seaweed within so short a distance of the financial centre of the world.

Long afterwards, when I had occasion to visit a firm of brokers—down-town brokers—being in the fortunate position after the death of my father of having money of my own to invest, I came fully to appreciate how completely removed from the rippling waves of concealed beaches were the thoughts of these argute, obtuse men, whose chief interest in life is juggling with money. I remember being shown into a kind of hall, where bidding was about to take place. In front of several rows of deep, leather-covered sofas was a large board, like those that tell of the arrival of trains in a station, with certain figures upon it. The market had not yet opened, but already there were men collected in groups, each with a cigar 'in his face', who periodically spat into the brazen cuspidors with which the room was proudly and ostentatiously furnished. And, by God, they did look like a bagful of foxes; and the more I observed their denaturalised, inhuman faces, the more uneasy did I feel with regard to my poor patrimony—so uneasy, in fact, that before I had spoken one word of business to anybody, I bolted down the elevator, and away over the hills; for I tell you, those boys looked to me as if they could pluck a Hallow-e'en goose as well as another—none better. What had impressed me as much as anything was the happy confidence these brokers obviously felt in life. Every word they spoke, every movement they made, if it was only to take a toothpick out of their waistcoat pocket, told how far they were from suspecting existence of concealing any dainty deceptions. Because they had had no hand in digging the trenches which brought the water from far-off springs to their nickel-plated cloak-room taps, because they had forgotten that each of their tight offices stood upon raw Manhattan rock, not so very far down underground, their vision of life, and the vision of life of their sons and daughters, had gradually become so divorced from the spirit of the quick earth that it was now practically impossible for them so much as to perceive the divine quiver capable of producing on the lawns of the Island of the Statue of Liberty, little white-clover flowers. To talk with the average business man is an experience not soon to be forgotten. These lickpennies have the mental development of a set of professional golf-players; why, the grey donkey under High Chaldon, which looks up now and then from its thistles to observe the weather signs, has infinitely more sense of existing than they! Most of them hardly realise they are alive, before their routine days, their routine thoughts, their newspaper-magazine-clubmen thoughts, come to an abrupt end, and they are carried away to a hideous vault, in a hideous cemetery, their coffins covered with ostentatious hothouse flowers, all wired together by commercial hands after the manner of a pagan rite which still lingers on, though with little meaning, into an age where even the grave is deprived of its dignity.

Sometimes we would visit Governor's Island, and from the other side of a prairie-like expanse, albeit from a much nearer position than the beach on the Island of the Statue of Liberty, look back at the city. I recollect once seeing it rise up from behind the hindquarters of a disconsolate, saddle-galled mule, which, with a sneering expression upon its smart, long-shaped face, stood in the near foreground, trying to bite, with aged, elongated teeth, at its own back-side. We would walk to the furthest end of the Island, where beyond a row of whitewashed posts we could sit down and watch the great liners steer for the open sea, with the music of a sea-bell in our ears, a sea-bell belonging to a buoy in mid-channel, which caused to come over the water a sound of distant sadness, as though, through fathoms of grey wintry depths we were hearing a dirge sung by mermen monks over the stiff fish-bones of a Neckan, who never, never again would sit upon a summer headland, 'the Baltic Sea along'. If we had more than a few hours, we would go to Staten Island and visit Prince's Bay. Here was a strip

of coast that in winter would be completely deserted.
Here we could walk along a real beach, under a cliff, toward
a lighthouse which stood on a hill by itself, with a lane
leading up to it from the shore—a lane, in the grass of
which, one afternoon, we found a quantity of toadflax, or
'dead men's bones', as the old lighthouse-keeper told us
he called them. This man's house was overgrown with ivy,
and each side of it, according to the way of the wind, was
used by sparrows for a roosting-place. Very happy I used to
be on cold winter afternoons, returning to a warm fire for
tea, carrying from this seaside cove some rare vignette in
my head, such as would have delighted Theocritus—the
picture of a fisherman, bent double, against a darkened sky,
pulling his net into a black boat—taken away in one's
memory like a charm against the affronts of modern life,
against the jarring clangour of the turnstiles on the elevated
railways, or the physiognomies of the Jewish lawyers, who
used to cluster about the soiled door of Jefferson Market
prison, like a flock of Pharaoh's chickens battening upon
corruption.

Once I visited this favourite seashore of Prince's Bay on
a summer morning. My brother was with me, and after we
had trailed along the edge of a hayfield, grown high with
tasselled flowering-grasses, we climbed down the cliff, to
find the beach strewn with the bodies of dead fish, done to
death apparently by some pernicious chemical or oil with
which the water had been contaminated. Indeed, right in
front of us we saw one struggling along at the top of the
water, upside down, like the fish that are depicted some-

times in the curling waves of old oil paintings, only in this case obviously taking its unnatural position not because of the approach of any dolphin-drawn chariot, but because of some frightful internal torment. Immediately John, in spite of all my protestations, advanced into the water, and standing with the sea up to his waist, made a series of clutches at the silver, slippery, exposed belly with his long, bony hands. Eventually, to my surprise, he actually did succeed in snatching it out of the water. After I had watched him kill it by banging its head against a rock, I persuaded him to reclimb the cliff and return to the hayfield, having no mind that we should spend all the precious hours of our day together retrieving these unfortunate creatures from their evil torment, especially since I would not have dared to eat any of them.

On other occasions, we visited the canal near Newark, a lovely, disused canal that now, alas, is to be drained and made into a speedway. I and my friend have walked by its banks at each season of the year; in springtime, when the pipers first began to call, their gay chirruping sounding from concealed places in each damp swamp, as though some-where, under the skunk-cabbages, amid the tinkling of sleigh-bells, little elves in their peaked winter caps were engaged in noisy, preoccupied barter on an April highway; in summer, when fishermen under shady trees angled for catfish, extraordinary catfish, whose spiked backs availed them little enough, pardi, when they once had a barbed hook in their upper lip. And in winter we would come there also, when all was deserted, and the snow lay crisp on the towpath, and it was possible to cross to the other side of the canal by sliding down white slabs of ice which rested against each bank, until we reached the middle, where all was level and sound.

Coincident with my discovery of Patchin Place came the bettering of my fortunes. *Ebony and Ivory* had been refused by Boni and Liveright, by B. W. Huebsch, by Knopf, by Seltzer, by the Sea-Gull Press, and I was at a loss to whom next to send it, until I suddenly remembered that Mr. Symon Gould, who had always, I knew, preserved a kind of romantic faith in my brother's genius, together with a suspicion that if properly directed it could be converted into 'yellowbacks', had lately become prosperous through the publication of a small handbook on Coué. Notwithstanding a certain lack of *finesse* in the amenities of social relationships displayed by this young Jew, I liked him. Had he not shown himself a man of no mean parts, in that, on one occasion, he had had the astounding temerity to over-reach no less a person than Mr. Frank Harris himself, just as an impertinent jackal might take a happy-go-lucky snap at the bum of some old man-eating lion with porcupine-quills in its paws? Indeed, Mr. Gould always put me in mind of a red-legged Palestine jackal, a wise Palestine jackal, who knew how to pad it past a thousand gins, were they covered with wild asses' dung never so cleverly, and was familiar likewise with each disused garden-pipe giving access to the vineyards of the Gentiles. I appeared with my manuscripts under my arm just when the sales of the Coué book were at their height, and when Mr. Gould, seated at a desk in a spacious office on Fifth Avenue, was seriously contemplating launching out into the publishing business. He accepted *Ebony and Ivory* out of hand, and within a month had the book printed and published, advertising and 'boosting' it with concentrated energy.

Merely to think of Frank Harris in association with Mr. Symon Gould was to me extremely diverting. Louis Wilkinson had some time before given me a letter of introduction to the old buccaneer, and I had had lunch with him at the Lafayette. Here was a man, looking like a race-course bookie, a company promoter, who was acquainted with every writer of his time; a man who had received into his round, tufted ears the intimate confidences of no less a person than Thomas Carlyle; who referred quite casually to the most formidable Frenchman of the last century as 'Guy'; and who, with the utmost gravity, confessed that at their first meeting, Walter Pater had not seemed to 'take to him much'. Sitting on the other side of a small round table, decorated with olives and hard red radishes, I was reduced to attentive silence, as one story succeeded another, interspersed with glances from under dark eyebrows that affected me like dagger-stabs. Yet how generous and courteous the old veteran was, standing for the charges of our luncheon and driving me back to my wretched house in a taxicab! And what vitality he had, this companion of Wilde's! His vitality alone amounted to genius. In spite of his bowler hat and his greatcoat lined with shabby fur— jackal's fur, perhaps—he belonged surely to another age, to an age more vital than ours. When I said good-bye to him, I felt I had been salting my celery with some Benvenuto Cellini, full of words and a divine fury. I found, too, that this impression was confirmed long afterwards, when the first volume of his autobiography fell into my hands; for in spite of the numerous lapses in literary tact with which the book abounds, I felt nothing but admiration for a man who could compose a volume of this kind and boldly sign his name to its title-page. I dare say there are others who would experience quite a different emotion after the perusal of its pages, but I for a great many years have held to the opinion that far from there being too many, there are too few erotic books accessible to the ordinary reader. I think when the mood is upon us we should be allowed to read *just what we like*. It is a fact to be noted, and perhaps to be regretted, that one soon becomes sated with reading pornography, and for this reason I can see no cause or just impediment why we should be deprived of such harmless personal diversions, when on rainy afternoons we climb up into the apple-loft, tired with playing battledore and shuttlecock in the schoolroom. The way we Occidentals plot to prevent one another from enjoying some of the most childish and natural amusements of life has always amazed me. I suppose those in authority, for the most part men of substance obsessed by the possessive impulse in one form or another, wish to keep this river of subterranean radium as much in control as possible, lest it should seep up through the stones of their cellars and set their money-boxes afloat, and there would presently be found nobody to sit on their revolving stools and assist them in their predatory enterprises. For myself, I like upon occasions to get hold of a good bawdy book; and I believe, if the spiritual health of the community were to be considered, that there are many turgid and insensitive minds, up and down the country, whose imaginations could only be roused by such gay Epistles to the Colossians.

CHAPTER FOURTEEN

Certain Celebrities

THE PUBLICATION of *Ebony and Ivory* and *Thirteen Worthies* had a very beneficent influence upon my days. I made no money out of them, but on the other hand I found it more easy to get my stories and essays published, so much so that I was presently able to move into Patchin Place, into the rooms that had just been vacated by Mr. Dudley Digges. I now, in order to get as much fresh air as possible, made a habit of doing all my writing in the little back-yard. As a place to work in it had only two drawbacks; the first of these being that a terrier dog was sent out there each morning, and these diurnal canine visitations gave the mould about the roots of the Ailanthus trees a most unpleasant smell that reminded me, when it reached my nostrils diluted by the air of the yard, of the smell of dry Osborne Biscuit crumbs. The second drawback was only in evidence during the hot summer months, when there was danger of my being distracted from the crafty composition of my prose by the proximity of a young lady, in a room opposite, who, with song and laughter and a dozen pretty postures, would dress by her open window. Fortunately for me the little slug-a-bed never woke till mid-day, so that I did have some hours each morning undisturbed by troubling glimpses of white fingers held to red lips, of white peeled-willow limbs.

I used to meet many literary people in Patchin Place. It was here that I saw Jules Romains for the first time, a true Frenchman if ever there was one. Only to watch him shrug his shoulders, only to watch the way he raised his eyebrows, as he took in, with genial relish, the separate sapidity of each new caller, was instructive. I can speak no French, so I was able to understand little or nothing of what he said; but later in the evening, as we sat opposite each other at Broad's, breaking up the shells of two lobsters, I certainly came to appreciate the delicacy of his mind, as it flitted, like a five-spotted burnet-moth, from one topic of conversation to another. He was a pacifist in the War; and we asked how he would have liked it if the Germans had been allowed to overrun France. 'Je ne l'aurais pas aimé du tout, mais j'aurais préféré même cela à la mort de trois millions de mes compatriotes.'

One evening I was invited by Theodore Dreiser to meet some friends of his. In the very centre of the room sat Dreiser himself, entirely ignorant of the fact that the guests he had brought together were not mixing well, and ready at a moment's notice to forget all of us as he followed the flounderings of his own wayward imagination, which, like a mammoth whale, with snortings and spoutings, plunged onward over the limitless ocean of life to the Isles of the Blest. Suddenly there entered upon us a youth, a little the worse for drink, whom everybody called Scotty, and who, I learnt afterwards, was the novelist, Scott Fitzgerald. There was something about this young man, who came in from 'Tough Man's Bend' with a bottle in his hand, that I liked extremely. He had evidently never met Dreiser before; and, far gone in his cups as he was, he addressed the elder novelist with maudlin deference. It was as though some young Dick Lovelace had come bursting into Ben Jonson's room; only, when one looked more closely at this boy's face, one noticed that it had a weak, pretty, blue-eyed, modern look that would have been curiously inappropriate in more heroic days. Mencken, Carl Van Vechten, and Ernest Boyd were among Dreiser's guests. I always had liked what I had heard about Mencken, but I never expected to meet anyone so squat, a veritable tweedledum, with curtailed, schoolboy jacket, making schoolboy jokes and talking schoolboy talk with a kind of boisterous *bonhomie*. Though I saw at a glance that his nature entirely lacked that finer edge which some of us perhaps rate too highly, I felt that there was no nonsense about him. I felt, in fact, that he was in possession of a far sounder intellect than, for example, that other zany of God's Nordic circus, Mr. G. K. Chesterton. Carl Van Vechten sat silent on a hard chair, his clever head drooping slightly to the left. Indeed, I have never been in the company of this famous wit when he did not appear to me to be drooping like an aging madonna-lily that has lost its pollen and has been left standing in a vase which the parlour-maid has forgotten to refill with fresh water. Yet this is not quite true either; for I do remember seeing him light up in the company of Miss Rebecca West at a certain *Dial* dinner, while we others sat in a doleful ring, like toads on toadstools, before two flashy fairies. Miss West seemed to me to be abusing her talent and orignality for the satisfaction of obtaining a reputation for 'smartness' in modish literary circles. But perhaps my rusticity, a certain agrarian quality in me, is of necessity averse to the kind of verbal levity, the clever bandinage, that seemed to come so readily to the lips of this clever lady and Mr. Van Vechten. 'A gloomy old fellow,' was how she dubbed me when somebody mentioned my name in her presence a year later.

To the right of Carl Van Vechten at this party in Dreiser's room sat Ernest Boyd, with his silky red beard well combed, feeling, as he told me, not 'very well'. I have always been disposed to respect this urbane, versatile translator. I always like the sound of his voice, soft as the voice of a wood-pigeon cooing over its two white eggs (wood-pigeons never have more than two white eggs) in its stick-nest below. I have always regretted that I never had an opportunity of talking for any length of time with him, but wherever I went I was sure to *hear* his voice. I remember hearing it suddenly over my shoulder, when under the eye of my generous host, I was doing my best, without any show of embarrassment, to select from a most confused, elaborate, and to me intimidating menu-card at the Century Club an appropriate luncheon. I remember that particular luncheon as having confirmed in me a prejudice that I have always felt against clubs, especially clubs of the more exclusive kind, where everybody is trying, as best he may, to live up to some objective standard of deportment which I suspect of having its origin, if its origin could ever be traced, in the fussy, exacting taste of some wretched head-waiter, who, if one deviates in the least **degree** from the rules accepted by his punctilious, spellbound mind, as, for instance, by ordering turnips with shad, raises a discreet left eyebrow, more alarming to the members of such institutions than the still small voice in a Syrian desert. I was led into the library of the Century Club to inspect the books there. How curious, in such a place, to see an edition of Poe's poems scrawled over with his own handwriting, to mark how he dotted his 'i's' with little complete circles, to observe all this, and actually to hold between one's fingers in the centre of this fortress of senile Philistines, so treasured a scrap of sublime imagination! I felt like a Celtic slave, who, with infinite care, was secretly preserving in his cupped hand a flake of sea foam blown into some great Roman seaside hall, where a sumptuous feast is in progress, because in his captivity it reminded him of the Atlantic and the wild cliffs of Wales.

It was at about this time that I met the two English novelists, Gilbert Cannan and Hugh Walpole. Hugh Walpole I only shook hands with, but I had an opportunity of watching him as he chatted society chat over his teacup to a roomful of admiring, but (our hostess excepted) quite peculiarly stupid, women. As soon as I was introduced, I remembered that I had sat next to him while attending history lectures at Cambridge—Walpole of Emmanuel, I remembered him quite well. I think there must have been something nicer about him in those days, for that afternoon I came to the conclusion that I did not like men of letters to be too plump or to possess too agreeable tea-party manners.

I certainly could not quarrel with Gilbert Cannan on

either of those scores; for when I met him, the dry old stationary heron kept looking about Paul Rosenfeld's room as though it were filled with birds of alien feather. 'Americans don't know what good manners are,' he said to my companion. 'And Englishmen don't know what bad manners are,' came back the very just retort. But however impatient one might grow with the air of intellectual superiority worn by him as naturally as the spats on his feet, one could not help respecting this lanky man, of whom Oscar Browning had predicted great things, long ago, in his rooms at King's. I talked to him about Africa, and it became very clear to me that he possessed the rare gallantry and magnanimity of temper which distinguish certain Englishmen, as, for example, John Galsworthy.

I remember this evening in Paul Rosenfeld's rooms particularly clearly, because when we stepped out into Irving Place it was snowing; and as we walked along Fourteenth Street, and down Fifth Avenue, I took the utmost delight in watching the flutterings of the myriad delicate unsmutched morsels, soft as the neck-feathers of Sam Hodder's white geese, and so light that their descent could be arrested by a single thread of my lady's hair.

CHAPTER FIFTEEN

The Salvation-Army Band

IT WAS sufficient merely to set eyes on Paul Rosenfeld to appreciate the diathesis of his personality. Plump as a grain-fed pheasant, he was a man of brave parts and deep culture. Like so many artists, he was extremely sensitive to criticism, but sensitive more perhaps on behalf of his friends than on behalf of himself. One had only to use such a phrase as 'inspired photographer' in connection with the name of Mr. Alfred Stieglitz, and he would 'go up into the air' as surely and rapidly as the lizard gardener in *Alice in Wonderland* shot up the chimney.

The Stieglitz group were always a source of entertainment to their friends. With their dedicated master marching on before, with 'The O'Keefe' to hand round a multi-coloured tambourine, with Mr. Marin, his wry lips to a trumpet, with Mr. Herbert Seligmann with his cheeks to the big bassoon, which in spite of all his blowing made no sound, and with Sherwood Anderson, the new convert, giving a heart-to-heart prayer at every market conduit, they pass down the great highway to an enviable immortality. Mr. Stieglitz, in his black cassock, conducting people round the rooms of the Montross Gallery, always put me in mind of Mr. Stucky, the loquacious verger of Sherborne Abbey, who, after a late meat-tea of toasted sardines, was used to discourse at large to travel-stained visitors on the flat flagstones of the Lady Chapel, under which, in his opinion, were concealed the royal bones of Æthelwulf, brother of King Alfred the Great. Mr. Stieglitz, it cannot be denied, knows his subject, and has done much to educate the citizens of New York City in the matter of modern paintings; but although he has the notable distinction of being the first American critic to appreciate Pablo Picasso, he has never, at any time, not even, one fears, as he sat warming his arctics over his celebrated stove in '291', realised that there are occasions in life when it is best to meditate upon the precious dust of kings in silence.

But however angry Paul Rosenfeld becomes on account of one's levity, one cannot really feel angry with him in return, for the simple reason that the man has a deep and generous heart, and this quite apart from the fact that he can write prose that has the effect of drawing the poison out of one's tail. Paul Rosenfeld's style has to be reckoned with. At its worst, it is true, it does remind one, as an amusing critic once suggested, of 'a merchant of Samarkand unrolling with slow deliberation sashes of silk', but at its best it carries one's imagination on strange flights. And how generous Mr. Rosenfeld is! How free with his money! Many an oyster, many a good duckling, have I eaten at his expense, at the Yale Club, or on one occasion at a Syrian restaurant, side by side with Mr. Stark Young, the grave critic of the theatre, who, as the seasons pass, comes more and more to appreciate the society of New York City, and who was once described to me by Mr. Reginald Pole, that

long-neglected ghost of Hamlet's father, as 'the leader of
the young intelligentsia'.

But not only has Paul Rosenfeld fed me, he has clothed
me also. When I was spending a winter in the Catskill
Mountains, where it was cold as the devil, he must needs
present me with two blankets, the finest, by God, that I
ever saw, made out of the wool of ewe lambs, gleaming-
white, and warm as polar-bear skins.

I once visited the Metropolitan Museum with him, and
he sat me down before an enormous Persian carpet. At
first I was as oblivious to its sumptuous appeal as any rook-
boy who had been brought in from a field of sprouting
barley; but gradually, as I sat there, looking at its silken
tapestried woof and at its intricate design of trees and
flowers, I came to understand something of the pleasure
that my friend was deriving from the silent contemplation
of so superb an example of patient craftsmanship. Truly, it
was as if no artistic achievement of the past escaped the
notice of this world-citizen who was acting as my gracious
monitor. It was as though the unique faculty had been given
him of evaluating, with a fine personal discrimination, every
piece of stone that has been chipped, every piece of wood
that has been carved, every piece of clay that has been
modelled, and every piece of cloth that has been woven
since our ancestors first separated themselves from the
animals. It was he who showed me the seven lion-headed
goddesses from Egypt! For nearly an hour we stood silent
before these monstrous antique monoliths, black goddesses
of granite, who held our two souls in a deadly clutch,

carrying them like bleating lambkins, into a darker and more sinister night than could ever have been imagined by the white-capped head of my kinsman, William Cowper. And yet there was something oddly voluptuous about these seven august sisters, with their protruding muzzles and naked paps, something that seemed to suggest that one's audacity might be rewarded with wyvern embraces of the most subtle kind, had one had the temerity to awaken one of them, to awaken the oldest of them from her sophisticated and protracted slumber, by placing a hand trembling with a horrid lust, on her fig-shaped knee.

Another celebrated critic whose personality I came to appreciate was Henry McBride. I used to meet him in the rooms of a very dear friend of mine in Washington Square. He would sit in a chair to the left of the fireplace, a chair always reserved for him, and as he took his tea he would delight the company with a flow of amusing observations, which kept skimming over the depths of existence with the same light assurance that a swallow shows as she dips her feathers from time to time in the mirrored surface of a duck-pond.

I had a very curious adventure one afternoon as I was approaching this same friend's rooms along Fourth Street. Shortly after I had left Sixth Avenue, I passed close by a man who was also advancing in the direction of Washington Square. Now it is a habit of mine, engendered, I surmise, by an insatiable, almost morbid curiosity in every stray personality that even remotely enters my sphere of observation, to peer with indecent concentration into the faces of people in the street. The lamps were not yet lighted; and for this reason, and because a damp, blinding snow was falling, it may have been that I looked into the countenance of this particular stranger with more than usual rudeness. I cannot say. I only know that my eyes encountered a physiognomy that affected me in a most startling manner. The tattered greatcoat, with little heaps of melting snow peaked up on both shoulders, might have sheltered the walking corpse of some enemy of mine, green from the grave, *who recognised me and whom I recognised.* Never in my life had I seen such evil features as those that looked up at me out of the mist, and yet it seemed to me that I knew them. I hurried forward, trying to assure myself as best I might that the look I had received was accidental, was, indeed, the customary look of this singular pedestrian. I had only two more blocks to go, but the faster I walked the faster padded the shuffling footsteps of my new acquaintance a few yards behind me. I could hear him talking. Was he talking to himself or to me? The whole demeanour of the man, the shape of his square, stooping shoulders, as I had observed them so indifferently from behind, seemed now horribly characteristic and as recognisable as the figure of one of those criminals one notices in the papers, whose spatulate fingers appear to have doomed them to the gallows from their mother's womb. But I was still uncertain whether, by some wretched chance, I had really managed to direct the venom of this extraordinary being against myself, when I drew near my friend's door. I ran hastily up the tall flight of steps and put my finger on the electric bell, moving aside, meanwhile, into a darkened recess. To my horror, I saw the figure of my pursuer stop short and look up into the shadowed alcove as though to assure himself that I had not yet got into the house. I remained perfectly motionless, but I knew that he saw me; and sure enough, a moment later, with lowered head, he began advancing up the slippery slabs. It was one of those moments in life when one's physical nerves acquire the taut intensity of nightmare nerves, and one's mind is driven out like a lost dog beyond the hurdled fold of ordinary commonplace experience. 'I'll rip your belly open with a knife,' I heard him snarl at me; but at the same instant, while he was still a few feet away, my fingers, which held the handle of the inner door, felt the first jingle of deliverance. I have always despised these doors that dispense with the services of a porter, that offer one entrance in such a tricky and absurd manner; but that afternoon the teasing rattle was as welcome to me as the dangling end of a rope to a man on the brink of a precipice. I slipped discreetly into safety. When I reached the room above, I told my story; but sitting there with the cozy on the tea-pot, and Henry McBride in his usual place, I despaired of conveying to the company the peculiar sensations through which I had so recently passed. Some of the guests perhaps in their courtesy to me, did rise and look out of the window. There below us the familiar green buses came swaying through the great arch, and people, *ordinary people*, were walking on the muffled pavement outside. Even to myself my story seemed the most utter folly, and my friends went back to their chairs and resumed their conversation.

Henry McBride was invariably charming to me, but I always felt that his mind, apart from its congenital frivolity, was cognisant and philosophic, was haunted, in fact, by the alarming suspicion that he himself and his room at the Herald Square Hotel, with its shining hot-water pipes, and, indeed, for the matter of that, 'the great globe itself' were merely balanced in the unsatisfactory manner of a spinning top that has to fall with a sidelong rush sooner or later, later or sooner.

CHAPTER SIXTEEN

The Poets

FEW PEOPLE that I met in America delighted me more than Padraic Colum. In the presence of this man, of this 'faëry cardinal', as my brother John once called him, I never failed to feel that particular spiritual elation which authentic poets are able to arouse in the hearts of those of us who value imagination more highly than anything else in the world. I could never set eyes on Mr. Colum without longing to go out into a cornfield to gather for him an armful of red poppies. I would long for an opportunity to do him the simplest service, to draw water out of a well for him, to carry him bowls of fresh cream, or to sit weaving for him a jacket from a new-shorn fleece, white as a cumulus cloud. Sometimes we met on Sixth Avenue, and, in a moment, while listening to his voice, I would forget the iron pilasters that upheld the clattering overhead railway, and be transported to places where toads with crinkled boxing-glove backs hop through long grass, or where the small, warm, western rains drift across the clumped whin-bushes of Ireland. On one occasion he described to me how, as a child, he had seen a begging fiddler leave a workhouse door on a March morning, with a white jackdaw sitting on his shoulder, and told me how wildly he had cried, because he himself, child as he was, wished to be stepping westward with a white bird. He also once related how, as a young boy, he came to write one of his most lovely lyrics, returning late, after a dance in an old farmhouse, to climb over the crooked limbs of a testy great-uncle in whose bed he slept, with his head full of his immortal melody. The company of Molly Colum delighted me also. She had a tart personality. If she had been born an Irish dairymaid, one could well imagine the retorts she would have tossed out of the loft-window, as she busied herself with the turning of yesterday's cheeses; for she had a tongue with a tang.

I recollect watching Mrs. Colum with great appreciation at a dinner-party given by Mrs. Murray Crane. At this same dinner there was a sister of our hostess, whose name I have forgotten, but whose distinction and spiritual poise made the deepest impression on me, made me feel, on leaving the house, as though we had come from breaking bread with some queen saint in ermine. And this sentiment was confirmed by the judgment of Edwin Arlington Robinson, in whose company I travelled back that night to Greenwich Village. Very clearly in my memory is fixed the picture of this stately man, with his 'mortis'd and tenon'd' reserve. Upon my soul, I never saw a poet so gifted who appeared less like a poet. His friend Ridgely Torrence used always to look to me as if he had just emerged from a grove on Mount Parnassus, his head crowned with a wreath of white bryony, while Mr. Robinson presented a front to the world suggestive of an uncommunicative gentleman of private means, who liked nothing so much as to sit down before a bright fire and read the *Life and Letters of Walter H. Page*, published by Doubleday, Page and Company.

Of all the poets I know, I think Richard Le Gallienne looks most like a poet. When *Ebony and Ivory* came out, I sent him a copy; and I shall never forget the thrill of pleasure it gave me when he came to tea at Patchin Place, carrying the book in his hand for me to inscribe. For Richard Le Gallienne always represented to my mind the last of the great figures of the Nineties; and, in truth, because of a certain look of fatality he wore over his shoulders, like Cæsar's cloak, one was constantly being reminded that one was talking with a man who had sat at meat with Swinburne, with Dowson, with Lionel Johnson, and with Oscar Wilde. In later days I used to walk with him in the Catskill Mountains, and have seen him many times come toward me with his jacket on his arm, light of step as any fisher-boy; but even then I never lost the impression, though we might be happy for long hours together, that in some curious way he was set apart, that he was hearing, from the hollow chasms of the great stone-quarries he loved, a voice I could not hear, seeing through the slim trunks of the silver birches which rose out of the bracken a form that I could not see.

Very different were the meditations roused in me by a glimpse I got of Bertrand Russell, that magnanimous philosopher, who had the air of some funny, eccentric eme of a noble family, who, once a day, at tea-time, would leave his turreted library to come down into the great hall to take a slice of thin bread and butter with the assembled house-party. He had been asked to dinner at Patchin Place; and because the green peas were still cooking on the gas-

stove, and the chicken ordered from the little French shop
next door to Bigelow's had not yet arrived when his taxicab entered the alley, I was instructed to entertain him for
a few moments in the room downstairs. I think he resented
the delay, fearing no doubt that he would be late in arriving
at some lecture he was giving that night; for, to my extreme
embarrassment, I saw him at one moment pull out his
watch, a movement that made me beyond words eager that he
should be set down, forthwith, before the young roasted
capon, which, with my left eye, I now saw pass the window.
In appearance Bertrand Russell resembled Sir Spencer
Ponsonby, while his voice put me in mind of the tired voice
of my cousin Ralph Shirley. I asked him whether he did not
consider the existence of America, with its successful
materialism and its stereotyped mob-thought, the greatest
menace to civilisation that the world had yet seen. He
replied that although it quite conceivably might become a
menace to our old-world conception of civilisation, he
thought there might emerge from it eventually, a new kind
of civilisation, a civilisation perhaps capable of producing a
greater amount of happiness for the human race than our
antiquated European values had ever done. He spoke, however, with diffidence, and when I asked him about the form
that such civilisation would take, he said he was unable to
tell, but suggested that I might look upon the invention of
the down-town skyscraper as a kind of symbol or token of
the future.

CHAPTER SEVENTEEN

The Publishers

IT WAS about this time that Mr. Symon Gould, of the American Library Service, suddenly announced to me that he intended to sell the rights of my books to some other publisher. *Black Laughter* had been planned, but not yet written; so I had before me the difficult task of persuading some one or other to back me to the tune of satisfying the uncertain claims of the American Library Service. My thoughts went at once to Mr. Alfred A. Knopf, who I knew was interested in the work of my brother, T. F. Powys.

I set out for his office. I had never quite got over my nervous dread of New York business buildings, and for this reason I omitted to consult the porter about the number of the floor I sought, but instead stepped briskly into a waiting elevator, trying to represent myself as best I could as a man who knew his business, by God, and had no time to waste. Immediately the door closed with a snap, and I found myself being carried aloft, my belly tingling as though my diaphragm had become suddenly porous to the winds of heaven. I asked the boy to let me out at Mr. Knopf's office. To my surprise and discomfiture he told me he did not know what floor it was on. I looked round the cage, in the hope of getting some help, for I knew everybody must have heard my question. It was now that my eye for the first time lit on an individual who seemed curiously to resemble Mr. Knopf as I remembered him, a dark, handsome man, who had the discreet, downcast eye and glossy look of an important Oriental official, who, after having witnessed the execution of Haman the son of Hammedatha, the Agagite, on a gallows fifty cubits high, was, in marabou-feathered sandals, hastening to present the King and Esther with a bouquet of Sharon roses. I was certain it was Mr. Knopf; but, when this same man quietly stepped out at the sixteenth floor without so much as a word or look, I was again not certain. There was nothing for it, therefore, but to be carried up to the twentieth floor, and from there down again to the ground floor, where, if the worst came to the worst, it would be necessary for me to consult one of those alarming alphabetical boards, merely to stand in front of which has invariably caused me in self-conscious embarrassment to forget my a-b-c's. When, finally, I stepped out at the sixteenth floor, and saw, seated in the sanctum of a spacious office, my companion of the elevator, and realised that in very truth I had been flouted by the great publisher himself, it required all the presumption of my exaggerated self-confidence to support me in presenting my cause to his clever and beautiful lady. I don't suppose I shall ever be able to obliterate from the tablets of my memory the peculiar sense of ignominy—perhaps entirely without cause or justification—I experienced as I descended that day down, down, down, as if under the very heels, soft as shammy leather, of this powerful business man, who so obviously wished to dissociate himself from me and my affairs.

During my stay in New York, I used greatly to enjoy working at the Public Library. On many a bright frosty morning have I turned into Fifth Avenue, trembling with a kind of secret exultation as I looked up at the narrow, Cubistic piles on each side of the famous thoroughfare, sharp-edged and gleaming in the early morning sunshine. Away I would walk, past the butterfly shop with the clouded yellow in the window, past Brentano's, till I found myself on the paved front of the great building under that absurd statue representing an insipid girl uneasily seated on a squatting horse, with the words, 'Beauty old but ever new, Eternal Voice and Inward Word', writ above her head—words that to the intelligence of any honest salesman of roasted chestnuts mean nothing at all, and might be taken, in fact, as a typical expression of that windy, high flying idealism which does so much harm in this world. How exhilarating it used to be to enter the reference-room of the great building, and to sit there reading the works of some old English worthy, surrounded by an accidental assemblage of men and women, boys and girls, who, with preoccupied, silent attention, were assimilating small scraps of wisdom from the books stored away with such care and method in the surrounding shelves!

On fine afternoons I would sometimes visit the Zoological Gardens in the Bronx. I used to like to come down the high stairs of the elevated railway, to pass the peanut men with their steaming kettles, and finally to go through the turnstile on the other side of the white gateway, and so to walk along an asphalt path till I came to where the bison

were kept. Here were preserved the last remnants of those
great herds that not so very long ago had wandered supreme
with wind-combed shoulders, over the prairies, herds
decimated by a race of terrifying mammals who, for the
amusement of their children, preserved a handful of them
alive in a tiny wired-in enclosure denuded of everything
but their own dung and a few bundles of hay. But, by God,
in this world it does not do to have too delicate a morality,
and I was well pleased to see the lions and the leopards
trotting up and down behind good sound bars. Had not I
often enough trembled at hearing their voices, as with
flaunting tread and eyes of flame they crossed from one
escarpment to another, ignorant that at last their hour also
had struck, and that they were about to be stamped out of
existence like so many obnoxious vermin? In this world it
is necessary to cultivate, to acquire, a tough attitude that
knows nought of fanciful misgivings. I used to look at Silver
King, the Polar bear presented to the gardens by Paul J.
Rainey, and envy the famous hunter his freedom from the
kind of imaginative sympathy that would have made him
feel upon his conscience, by day and by night, the restless,
troubled movements of the great animal, up and down,
up and down, which for his own personal amusement, he
had doomed to perpetual imprisonment.

Once, I remember, as I approached the aviary, I met Mr.
Jerome Blum, the artist. He had been inspecting the croco-
diles, those curious reptiles who spend their captivity
immobile as stones, and yet have that in their eye suggestive
of a sly knowledge that they and their kind will have little

or no difficulty in outliving the terrible régime of man. In spite of his grotesque appearance I always felt that Jerry Blum possessed in him something sublime, just as a toad carries a diamond in its head. I had stayed with him for a week once, in his house at Mount Kisco, and I shall never forget how inspired his extraordinary features looked, hideous as the features of a buck-baboon Cézanne, as he sat opposite me painting my portrait under an apple-tree. There was a bathing-pool at the bottom of the orchard; and at mid-day we would run down to it, and I would sit on the bank amongst the long grasses and dragon-flies, watching the heavy shoulders of my friend protrude from the water, till his uncouth flounderings would disturb from the rushes a bittern that would rise into the air and float away over the old mill, over the distant woods.

It was always a relief to me to enter the bird-house in the Bronx. Perhaps Leopardi is right, and birds are the only creatures upon the earth who are really happy, their superficial frivolity seeming to be exactly adapted to something heartless, shifty, and unprincipled at the back of life. I certainly used to feel this most strongly when, upon pushing open the doors, my ears would be assailed by the shrill, high-pitched insistent screams of these extraordinary vertebrates that have learnt to raise themselves from the ground with the amazing buoyancy of moths and butterflies. Yet how lovely to see the bird of paradise display itself to its paramour, quivering with outstretched wings, as though even in a sandy-floored cage it could catch the exact vibration of the music of the spheres!

I used also to like to visit Prospect Park in Brooklyn. It was pleasant to walk across wide stretches of soft grass, with a distant background of green trees. Sometimes I would find my way into the Quaker graveyard and sit down amongst the unassuming tombstones of these good people, with my heart full of love and my head full of gentle thoughts. And there came an occasion when I certainly was in need of such benign influences. It happened one day that I saw walking in front of me two children, a girl of fifteen and another much younger. The elder of the two children, a beautiful creature with long whip-cords of golden hair hanging down her back, was evidently bullying her friend. She was holding her tightly by her wrist, but I could not hear what she was saying. As I passed, she shot a glance at me over the head of her victim, a glance inquiring, subtle, full of meaning, as though she wanted me to understand what was going on, and felt confident that she had only to look at me in *a certain way* for me to become forthwith a tacit accomplice in her ill-behaviour, ill-behaviour from which she was obviously deriving an intense neurotic excitement. Although I am by nature extremely indulgent to all sexual irregularities, and indeed consider such tolerance essential to the graces of a civilised gentleman, I have sometimes allowed myself to entertain misdoubts as to the propriety of what is known to the world as sadism. What, I have asked myself, is this unregenerate emotion doing in our Christian era, this emotion that takes so wild and unreflective a delight in stripes and tears? Now, when this attractive little monster, with hair like golden whip-cords hanging down to the

small of her back, looked at me in this odd way on the great
lawn of Brooklyn's park, my heart leapt up in eager re-
ciprocity, and I simply could not show any disapproval, no,
not even when, dragging her small companion on to the
grass, she began, with a cold, ambiguous smile, to smack
her bare legs. I looked at her, just as in Africa I had looked
at a naked boy and girl torturing a white-breasted hawk,
and then fled away. Had not I been stung by a poisoned
snake, with marvellous Picasso-like markings on its back,
and was it not imperative for me just then to reach the
artificial lake, nay, to sail over its glassy surface, in a flat-
bottomed boat designed to look like a swan?

Sometimes, with my sister Philippa, I would walk east-
ward along Tenth Street, till we came to the river, and
there, on a bleak wharf, with the gasworks behind us making
periodical explosions, we would sit for hours together
looking over the grey waters of the East River. After
the streets through which we had just been walking, streets
swarming with life like the under side of a stone, it was
wonderful from so secure and deserted a position to look
out at gulls and sailboats and free, ocean-travelling ships.
For how indescribable these streets that lay behind us were,
noisy, crowded streets, with coster-carts along each curb,
coster-carts from the sides of which strange, raggle-taggle,
gypsy-like Jews, Jews who combined the fury of so many
Jeremiahs with the craft of so many turbaned Jacobs, were
intent upon selling their wares, upon selling coloured
garments, or coloured fruit, or chunks of pickled watermelon of a faint-green hue, which tainted the air of the side-

walk with a taint bitter, astringent, aromatic, as the smell
of the streets of Aleppo! Here indeed was life, strident and
unappeasable! I saw one lusty fellow, with a great buggerly
black beard and a roving bull's eye, hold up a live eel. He
kept tapping it on its head to make it open its mouth, crying
out all the time, 'He alive, he fresh, he alive, he fresh!'
Good Lord, what a clatter and hubbub and turmoil these
streets manifested! What pestilence, or dire visitation, or
dire exploitation, could reduce the spring and rebound of
such eel-eaters? I saw in an undertaker's window a child's
coffin, padded with white satin a little dusty at the edges;
but well I knew that for every patient, waxen image carried
away in such a receptacle, there would be at least three
others to take its place. For on every step and stairway, and
at every window, there were mothers with whey-white
mammæ, suckling their young.

That winter the famous prophet and magician, Gurdjieff,
appeared in New York, accompanied by Mr. Orage, who
was acting for him like a kind of St. Paul. My sister had
been interested by what she had heard of the Institute at
Fontainebleau, and also by what she now saw of the perform-
ances of the pupils. She persuaded us one evening to go to
the Neighbourhood Playhouse to see them. On this night I
had an opportunity of observing Gurdjieff while he stood
smoking not far from me in the vestibule. He had a high,
bald head, with sharp, black eyes. His general appearance
made one think of a riding-master, though there was something about his presence that affected one's nerves in a
strange way. Especially did one feel this when his pupils

came on to the stage, to perform like a hutchful of hypnotised rabbits under the gaze of a master conjurer.

Orage came to tea at Patchin Place one afternoon and discoursed very lucidly and very wisely upon many obscure matters that had to do with the theories of the new cult. But I felt that nothing he could say could make me believe, so rooted were my two feet, even to my own satisfaction, in the heavy soil of the flower-growing, dung-strewn earth which knows nought of ghosts. Yet I could not fail to be impressed by the conclusions come to by this most brilliant philosopher, whose mind is so vehemently set upon rejecting any black-handed behaviourist theory of life, a philosopher looking like a boy in Dr. Arnold's Sixth Form at Rugby, who had found, beyond all expectation, a rare, white-plumed pigeon in his ink-stained desk.

CHAPTER EIGHTEEN

The Rocky Mountains

IT WAS in the spring of 1924 that I was invited by Dr.
James S. Watson, of *The Dial*, to join him on an
expedition into the Rocky Mountains. This man had
always delighted me. It used to amuse me to watch him
drifting through life with the unresisting adaptability of a
long, drooping straw caught in the current of a lively trout-
stream. He was enormously rich, and yet liked to appear
poor. He was extremely wise, yet preferred to be thought
foolish. With a small black bag, held in the long, sensitive
fingers of an artist, he was to be encountered on a perpetual
drooping peregrination through the side-streets of Greenwich Village. He made one think of those silent, evasive
eels one hears about, eels that find their way to the ocean
from remote ponds, sliding their sinuous bodies through
night-dusky, dew-drenched pastures. He possessed a subtle,
cynical mind, which he did all in his power to conceal. He
was an extremely able doctor, who never practised, an
extremely clever writer, who never wrote. Whether one
met him in the French pastry-shop, or in the hall of his
house, with its mullioned window and noble stone chimney-
piece, he ever remained aloof and uncommitted. Even the
gracious presence of his beautiful lady at the end of a
lighted dinner-table was never sufficient to overcome his
embarrassed diffidence, a diffidence that seemed to cover

the most inconvenient reticences. In truth, as he knocked off the grey ashes of his cigarette, between the courses, on to the rim of the silver candlestick opposite the place where he sat, he was capable of interjecting some whispered comment that would completely destroy one's confidence and would keep recurring to one's mind for days afterwards, because of its teasing ambiguity.

To see Dr. Watson and Mr. Scofield Thayer together was something to remember. It would have required a Henry James to tabulate and record each interesting tarot card of this astounding association. And yet these two young men, in the face of the crass stupidity of the Philistine world, in the face of the sneering hostility of a score of pseudo-literary cliques, have managed to produce in America a journal which, without any doubt, is the most distinguished of its kind to appear in the English language since the publication of the *Yellow Book*. But how quaint it was to see these two working together for the æsthetic enlightenment of the Western world! It was like seeing a proud, self-willed, bull-calf bison, fed on nothing but golden oats, yoked to the plough with a dainty, fetlocked, dapple-grey unicorn, who would, an' he could, step delicately over the traces and scamper to the edge of the prairie, where, under the protective colouring of a grove of pale wattle trees, he might be lost to the view of the world.

The taste of Scofield Thayer was the austere aristocratic taste of a Roman noble, of a Roman connoisseur, who has filled his marble hall with the work of his Greek slaves; while the Doctor's taste was that of a super-subtle Nicodemus who had a mania for collecting at night, by proxy, images of unknown gods, put together by indigent artists whose lack of rice was never for long out of the mind of this generous young man.

A rare happiness it was for me to find myself once again heading for the wilderness, with a stout pony under me, and half-a-dozen crafty, long-eared mules following, one behind the other, between the dark resin-smelling tree trunks. The first day, we rode thirty-five miles and camped in an open place a few hundred yards from the banks of a mountain lake. I was tired and lay down to sleep early. Just before dawn broke, I was waked by the howl of a timber-wolf. He uttered a single yell; and the lone cry had scarcely died down when a dozen elk, with cowslip-coloured buttocks, came cantering through the ghostly white light. As the sun rose I was walking by the edge of the lake. I shall not soon forget its beauty, with its two sections lying there like the gleaming, outstretched wings of an enormous purple butterfly. In appearance and shape the lake was not unlike Lake Elmenteita, and I found myself instinctively scanning its surface for the head of a hippopotamus. Across the sky, against an outline of snow-capped mountains, flew three white pelicans, their pouched beaks giving them a gross look, very different from that of the flamingoes I used to disturb at such an hour in Africa, with their rose-red wings and serpentine necks.

The Doctor left camp early on his quest for grizzly bears, while I, half an hour later, taking a rough stick in my hand, set out by myself. For some time I kept close to a riverbank. There were a great many willows growing there, but it was easy to push one's way through them. Suddenly I realised that some large animal was moving along on the other side of the stream. I sank down and waited. The creature was evidently working up my way. On it came, till, looking through the screen of narrow leaves, I could see a bull moose, with a cow behind him. If I had not seen their heads I would have taken them for rhinos, so massive and dun coloured did their flanks look, as they slowly advanced, browsing upon the fresh twigs. Presently the bull stepped into the moving water. I thought at first that he was going to head straight for my hiding-place; however, to my no small relief, he selected for his landing a spot some twenty yards further up-stream. He looked very imposing as he stood in the middle of the noisy water, with his head half turned to see if his cow was following. I saw him lift his tail, letting his dung fall splashing into the water with the extraordinary aplomb of a large grass-eater who is untroubled and undisturbed. He looked to me about the size of a bull eland, though perhaps not quite so tall. The spread of his horns in the bright sunshine was wonderful, but what a weight for the animal's great head to support —for that huge, ungainly head, with its prehensile upper lip.

I was back in camp by the evening. The trapper we had with us was a small, wiry man, who had been living in these mountains for years. He had the wary, wizened look of a marten which had been caught half a dozen times, and half a dozen times got itself free. It was interesting to watch his face. It remained dull and unresponsive in ordinary conversation; but the moment his senses were assailed, its expression changed to one of intense alertness. Again and again I saw him stand motionless, snuffing the air long before the rank smell of elk was apparent to us; and I have seen him stop, with ears pricked, when he alone was able to hear a bear at work on a piece of ant-infested timber half a mile away.

The next morning I again set out alone. It seemed to grow hot, with an almost tropical heat; and coming to a stream in the forest, I took off my clothes and slipped into a pool. I felt as naked and unprotected under those great silent pine trees as I had felt naked and unprotected in Africa, when I bathed in a certain hot spring overshadowed with leaves large as the ears of elephants. And not ten yards away I saw my first track of a grizzly bear, tracks far larger than those of a lion, more like the footprints of a man, only with claws instead of toes. I was glad enough to leave the dangerous place.

On my way back I came upon some beaver-dams in the flat near the river. I examined them closely. They were so solidly constructed that I was able to walk across them, though there was deep water on both sides. I put up a wild grey goose that went sailing away over the stone expanses, over the heaps of white skeleton-like timber which the snow-floods had left stranded. I was fascinated to see how the beavers had contrived to bring trees down from a quaking-asp grove by means of a canal they had dug. I looked with awe at the marks of their webbed feet in the soft mud, the footprints of a warm-coated people possessing the ingenuity of goblins.

After some days we reached the Great Divide. Here was a river which separated itself into two halves, the waters of the one half being destined to reach the Atlantic Ocean, while the waters of the other would eventually flow into the Pacific. I knelt at its fork, and with my right hand drank from the one, and with my left hand drank from the other. There were so many trout that it was possible to beat them on to the banks with sticks, and we spent an hour at this merry pastime. I tell you it was something to see our trapper Jones slit them up ready for supper! Their entrails he let fall on the dry, round pebble-stones at his feet; and Watson pointed out to me that their hearts still continued to flutter, even as filthy offal. I picked up a heart, a small, pink quivering morsel of flesh, that refused to die. It was like a baby skate.

When we next moved, we rode over the flat top of a mountain which reminded me of that part of the Aberdare range in East Africa where the elephant trails cross between the Milowa and Sugeroi Rivers. Coming down from the mountain we saw a brown bear. A little further on I caught sight of a porcupine absorbed in its own secret pursuits, and yet cognisant of our presence. What an infinite complacence its concentrated attitude seemed to suggest! And yet it is ordained that even a porcupine's composure is sometimes ruffled, as, for instance, when a bear turns it over on its back and gravely begins to rip open its unprotected, bark-filled, grass-filled stomach. The next morning

I walked down a creek, and then along the foot of a mountain. I came upon a great deal of sage-brush. I kept picking it as I walked and crushing it in my fingers. How the plant, with its gnarled, lavender-like growth, its dry odour, health-giving and aromatic, must appeal to people born in the West of America, so redolent it seems of the dust, and prairie-dogs, and hot stones, and perpetual sunshine of their open plains!

I walked under a cliff clustered over with the nests of mountain swallows, which projected from the rock like so many Kikuyu gourds. Many of the nests were built so low that I found it possible to look down their funnels to where the small feathered mothers were sitting with sharp eyes full of apprenhesion. Meanwhile, a hundred screaming male birds flew backwards and forwards about my ears, a veritable hail-storm of darting arrowheads. In the Rocky Mountains I was always impressed by the chatter and noise made by small creatures, the tiniest squirrel taking upon itself to shout after me. In Africa they would have soon learned better, would soon have learned that to make the world aware of one's presence is a privilege belonging to the carnivore, and not to little, thrifty nut-collectors. One day I climbed to the top of a mountain. I sat on a rocky ledge on its very summit, overlooking a wide, tree-grown valley. A thousand feet below me, and yet far enough above the tops of the trees, two eagles swept backwards and forwards in wild pursuit of each other. Aha! What a love-making was that! I began to retrace my steps; and there, right in the open, near a snow-drift, I came upon a bitch badger with three young ones. I tried to get close to her, but she faced me down with many false advances and ugly growls. The little badgers were round and very fat, and were covered with fur of a reddish colour. I came down the southern side of the mountain. For half an hour I rested upon a jack-pine at the top of a sloping shell-rock precipice. A moose-bird came and mocked at me; and a chipmunk, with tail erect, eyed me suspiciously, squatting upon its hind legs like a miniature kangaroo. These cloudy coloured streams above the timber-line, caused by the melting snow, are not much to drink at; and I was glad enough to come upon a spring of pure water, which spouted out of the side of the hill. I knelt down and drank at the earth itself, as though I had my lips to the udder of a monstrous, sweet-smelling, round-bellied dairy cow. The spring presently became a brown stream, which ran rippling through a grassy glade, green as the back of a green parrot. I lay down to rest, leaning over to look at the bottom of a clear pool, to look at the incredible activity taking place in its loose mud. Caddis-worms crept from mound to mound; and strange centipedes, with earwig tails, paraded over the shining subaqueous pebbles. I watched them as if I were looking into an aquarium. What did these creatures, with their remote, intense, intimate life, know about eagle love-making, or about bitch badgers, or about the moose that had dropped its flat horn not far from where I lay, a horn already nibbled out of shape by a porcupine? As I walked through these slippery pine-forests, I continually met with hot puffs of wind, pungent with the incense that rose from the sun-dried needle floor. But on the high lawns, where the lupin bloomed, the air was perfumed with the scent of flowers. If I shut my eyes, it was as though I were loitering in the kitchen-garden at home, between rows of divers-hued sweet peas. And how silent these uplands were, when the wind was still! Surely, if one had listened, one could have heard each tiny petal fall, could have heard the fanning of the butterflies' wings, as they flickered from one sweet-smelling blossom to another through the pollen-laden air.

One day I got to the top of the highest of all the mountains. Far above me I would see a waterfall sparkling in the sunshine, but when I reached it, there would be others still further up. Once on its summit, I followed along its razor edge, marvelling at the depths of the canyons that fell away on both sides.

The idea came to me that it might be possible to find another way down, and presently, looking over a banked-up snow drift, I fancied that if I followed the course of a stream which, from where I was standing, showed like a thin strand of silver wire twisting between the rocks, I should have small difficulty in reaching the timber-line, whose slopes seemed to fall away in easy gradations to the valley below.

Down I went, down over loose rocks, down over mud-slides, down through ridges of melting snow, till I reached the stream I had observed. Below one of its waterfalls I came to a hidden, mossy bank, where heather grew. So enchanted was I by the lovely seclusion of the spot that I lay down and rested for a few moments. Presently the sky became overcast, and a distant growl of thunder reminded me that I had better be starting once more on my descent. With considerable difficulty I slid from projecting rock to projecting rock, until I came to a place where the stream, gathering itself into one swift, deep channel, disappeared round the slippery, blackened base of an enormous boulder. Obviously I must climb over this obstruction. I clambered up its side and found myself looking into the empty cleft of a shocking precipice! Fearful lest my very movements might topple the boulder down into the void gulf, I slid back. On every side ugly bastions beetled above me. The mountain had become darkened. Black clouds, ragged as the wings of misshapen ravens, were racing across the firmament, clouds that looked as if they had been torn and fractured by too close contact with the wild landscape over which they were drifting. Crouched behind the granite block, with the water racing past my boots toward the treacherous crevice, I became terrified. My kneebones shook. Above me, ledge above ledge, the mountain towered. The least movement I made seemed fraught with danger.

Then, just as when I had been caught by fire in a tropical forest, a deep animal instinct of self-preservation became fully awake. Step by step, I climbed back by the way I had come, up over the slide, up past where the heather grew, up over the ledge by means of a fallen tree, up over the shell-rock where the woodchuck had called to me. Often I was compelled to rest for want of breath, but I would soon be on my feet again, climbing higher and higher, with the persistent deliberation of a bear who knows that a trapper without pity is after him. And now the great forest trees on the slopes of the mountain had become suddenly articulate. Exhausted, and soaked to the skin, I passed between their stark trunks, nervous, impotent, while far above me they moaned to each other, as their stiff arms bent and swayed in the rushing gale.

When I woke the next morning I looked out on to rain-drenched mountains that smelt like Africa in the rainy season. Through the open door of my tent I could see a porcupine feeding, drawing into its mouth great, wet leaves with its right paw.

The next week we moved into even wilder country. On all sides of our camp, jagged crags projected into the sky, their shoulders cusped with snow, their broad backs covered with shell-rock. At the timber-line there were a few scattered groups of fir trees, which used to appear to me as I rode in the valley below, like cloaked women, like desperate female fugitives in tattered green capes, who, in an evil hour, had been caught on the bare hillside, as they fled from some unprecedented disaster, to be petrified for ever, with drooping shoulders and bowed heads. How many black, merciless blizzards must it not have required to bend this timber into such uniform dejection! Once more I scaled a mountain-side; and as, from the summit, I scanned the wild prospect of the Rocky Mountains, I felt rise within me a pæan of triumph at seeing stretched out in every direction before my eyes this great ridged backbone of the world, which, sharp as the spine of a shark, each twenty-four hours in the diurnal revolution saws its way through the planet's circumambient atmosphere.

One night I sat for long hours over our camp-fire, the outlines of the distant mountains standing out clearly against the night sky, the trees that edged their slopes appearing like a growth of beard on a dead giant's chin. The red flames danced and the smoke drifted off into the surrounding darkness. I gazed at the glowing core of a burning pine-stump and tried to imprint the scene upon my memory. How emphatic and incontestable it all looked! The lively scarlet flames, the white snow, the encircling shadows! When I, at length, lay down in my blankets, I had a very curious dream. I dreamed that, as I was showing my brother Willie this country, we suddenly passed through a small door, and found ourselves back in the top orchard of our home in Somerset. My brother scanned the familiar fruit-trees in interested silence, the golden pippin, the russet by the terrace gate. He noticed the fresh gaps in their rows. I did my best to reassure him, though well I knew that time had done its work. Then it was that, while in my dream my heart sank with unutterable dismay at this new evidence of life's fatal instability, a long, low howl went moaning under the aged apple-trees, moaning across the lawns of the garden, moaning over the chimneys of the old house. It was a most singular howling, a howling such as one might fancy issuing from the contracted throat of a shackled god. It rang through my ears. Surely it could be no illusion. I sprang up from the ground wide awake. A coyote was making the creek echo with its barking, somewhere out in the darkness, beyond the smouldering fire. For nearly half an hour I lay listening to its dolorous voice.

Our last night in the mountains arrived. We were camped in a meadow-like valley by the side of a mountain river. The moon was full, I could not sleep. Slowly she moved from behind the mountains across the sky. Hour after hour followed, and still the austere beauty of that midnight scene arrested my consciousness. There, far above the chill, black, ossified mountains, above the motionless spears of the pine-trees, paraded the passionless, treacherous, immortal planet. And as I lay with my head resting on the meadow lupin, already cool with night-dew, I became aware at last of the consolation that is to be drawn from silent communion with matter, with Eternal Matter, bereft of divine innuendoes, but capable still of sustaining, after its sublime manner, the fearful and wavering soul of man. In the small hours of the night I rose up from where I lay, and with a blanket over my shoulder wandered along the river's shelving bank. To my left, in the centre of the drenched white pasture, I could see the dark shadow of the tethered mule, of the mule we called Ben, standing with ears forward, silently alert to all my movements while before me, between the charmed forest trees, lay the silver highway of the river, as magical and uncertain as life itself.

CHAPTER NINETEEN

Followed and Followed After

ONCE OUT of the mountains, it was with ravenous hunger that I ate my first salad at a wayside house. I devoured lettuces and radishes and spring onions with the same savage, unthinking ferocity that I have seen displayed by humpbacked cattle in Africa, when after months of being deprived of salt they would rush down to the 'lick' on the shore of the lake. For now that the strenuous expedition was over, I began to feel certain misgivings lest I had given my insistent pursuer a chance of overtaking me. As I sat, with hooked knee, in the small, sun-baked, grassless yard, twenty miles from Cody, I became more than ever convinced that the bacilli put to sleep by Abrams' magic had come awake again. By the time that we had arrived at Buffalo Bill's famous hostel, I was certain of it. I remember lying in a little upstairs bedroom, haunted by evil premonitions, while at intervals, through the open window would come floating in the voices of two young men who were emptying garbage. The stairway outside my chamber was adorned with innumerable oil-paintings of the gallant rough-rider, representing him as the central figure of a hundred adventures; Buffalo Bill engaged in a bloody battle with Indians, Buffalo Bill casting a lasso over the horns of a galloping steer, Buffalo Bill in a lonely, snow-covered glade standing over an elk. I could not but envy the fellow his lanate imperial beard, his brave demeanour, and his sound reins.

In the evening I walked as far as the equestrian statue of him, which, executed by Mrs. Harry Payne Whitney, now stands in a hot plain above the Shoshone River. I tapped one of the raised hoofs of the horse, and it gave back a tinkling, hollow sound. Meanwhile, the sun dropped beneath the rim of the distant mountains, transmuting the sagebrush into an enveloping Aztec chasuble of flashing phœnix feathers.

I reached New York on a Sunday evening. Never did I love the city so well. As my train drew across the Jersey flats, I felt the deepest possible allegiance to this metropolis of concrete and steel and glittering glass, refractive and indurate as a cleft diamond set in silver. It had been a hot day, and the streets wore that silent, deserted appearance which is characteristic of them on Sundays, when for a few hours the city's eager population pauses from its work, some to dip tired limbs in the sea, some, with knapsacks on their shoulders, to explore the recesses of the Palisades, some to loll out of high tenement windows, and others to sport together in closed, semi-dark chambers.

The day after my arrival, I accompanied my brother John to Garden City, to visit the publishing-house of Doubleday, Page and Company, in connection with his new novel, *Ducdame*. I had grown a great red beard in Wyoming, and I dare say I presented to the passer-by a sufficiently rough appearance. When we reached the Pennsylvania Station we found we had an hour to wait, and we therefore began wandering along the street in the direction of Ninth Avenue. Presently we came opposite a high brick wall, surrounding, so we surmised, a garden belonging to some Catholic institution. Beset as we were by the clang and clatter of the city, we both found something peculiarly pleasing about this quiet, unobtrusive brick wall, which hid, we hardly doubted, flower-beds of gold-dusted snapdragons and cool-budding dahlias. While looking at it I became conscious of a sudden weariness, and sank down where I was, on the edge of the curb. There was nothing in this action of mine to alarm or surprise my brother, and without a word he went over to a green receptacle for papers, and selecting the cleanest he could find, brought it back for me to sit upon. He then proceeded to walk up and down the street like a sentry, his black, forked figure 'in its dark cloud making its moan'.

The midsummer sunshine poured down upon me, and upon the convent wall, and upon the gleaming brass hames of the dray horses which kept rattling past. All at once, as I sat there, with my elbows resting on my knees, I became aware of a woman standing before me. I looked up, and at the same moment she handed me a coin that had upon it the delicate impress of a bison. For a fraction of a second I hesitated, and then I blessed her, blessed her as any real beggar might have blessed this unknown human being, who had manifested in so contrite a way the pity she felt for mortal suffering. And as I put the small coin in my trousers pocket, and watched my benefactress turn the corner where my brother was standing with folded arms, I felt for once completely reconciled to the human race, which, with all its selfishness and crude avarice is capable of producing, now and again, here and there, sometimes amongst the rich, sometimes amongst the poor, certain choice and magnanimous spirits, whose charity falls upon the heads of the undeserving with the softness of spring rain.

It was, I think, the day after this incident that I had occasion to visit my savings bank, at the corner of Fourteenth Street. In the time of my extreme poverty, I had selected this building as a suitable place for storing the few dollars I had in my possession. Often and often have I sat on its cheap bench, waiting for my name to be called through the iron meshes of the teller's window, indolently watching the pigeons as they fluttered from one Corinthian column to another on the further side of a dusty skylight, built to admit shafts of gold from a far distant sun, shafts or gold which would illuminate, like monks' folios, the enormous ledgers over which the young clerks bent their heads. And upon these occasions it was as though I had been privileged to pry into the squeaking, grinding, ill-fitted machinery that keeps the present system of society going, a machinery, surely, far less cleverly designed than the sidereal clock, invented by the Glastonbury monk, Peter Lightfoot, in 1320, which, with wheel and cog intact, still marks out the passing of minutes, months, and years, for the happy burghers of Wimborne Minster, in the ancient county of Dorset. I would review the long lines of patrons as they presented their soiled books, some to put money in, some to take money out. What curious expressions one saw on the faces of these human beings, on the lined, harassed faces of these men who had forgotten how to hunt, or to fish, or to grow corn, or to catch wild fowl, but who depended for a livelihood on procuring grubby scraps of paper, embellished with the countenances of clean-shaven or bearded Presidents long since dead! How the hands of the poor wretches would tremble and shake, as though with an ague, as they gathered up their money, too intimidated even to count it under the supercilious scrutiny of the petty recorders, who proudly took the part of pale-faced puppet judges in the degrading struggle!

That day, as I left the building and was crossing the street, in front of Uncle Ben's pawn-shop, I felt a sudden sharp stabbing pain under my right shoulder. It was the kind of pain that demands attention, that cannot be ignored, and when I reached Patchin Place, I found that I had a high fever. I left New York for the country that very afternoon. I suppose the journey into Connecticut had been nearly half completed when I realised by a certain familiar impediment in my breathing that I was going to have a hæmorrhage. I sat as still as I could, 'freezing'. It availed me nothing. Every few seconds I could feel my lungs filling with blood; and to breathe at all it was necessary for me to cough little, short, choking, coughs. I kept my head turned towards the window, and as best I could hid my face behind my hands. Slowly the pleasant, grey-walled Connecticut fields slid past my vision, already heavy with milkweed and golden-rod. The mere suspicion that I was really *this time* going to die put me into a state of deepest misery. I could not bear that my hour should be yet. I yearned for life as a dace with a barbed hook in its gullet yearns to be switching a free tail under Pye Bridge, upstream, with its companions.

All that night, as I lay on my back on a wide balcony, this same obsession was upon me. I could in no way accommodate my mind to the conception of Death. Let it be for others, but not for me. 'My life, O Lord Jupiter, only my life!'

For close on two months I rested where I was, and slowly, very slowly, felt my vigour return to me. Then I grew strong enough to walk in the garden, fragrant with ripening purple grapes, grew strong enough to observe the movements of a spider, who, with delicate, precise hands, was suspending his symmetrical web between a coxcomb and a nasturtium leaf; grew strong enough to raise my head and pass the time of day with a young woman who was looking out of a window, and whose face, half hidden by a stooping sunflower, was pale as a rain-washed autumn mushroom, for no better reason than that she had a cancer and was to be dead and buried before the first fall of snow.

CHAPTER TWENTY

Montoma

WITH MY consumption once more upon me, it seemed the utmost folly to resume my life in New York City; and now that my actual struggle for bread and meat had been relieved, I decided to spend the winter with my companion in the Catskill Mountains.

We rented a small farmhouse, situated on the top of a winding mountain road. We moved in at the time when it was impossible to walk at night down a lane without being deafened by the shrill cacophony of katydids. With their green wings concealed behind the green leaves of the hedge-row trees, these singular insects made music to one another. As we stumbled over dry, dead sumach-sticks—sticks that we were to collect later on for firewood—as we brushed with our ankles tufts of scented fern on our way to this or that deserted quarry, we would feel like clumsy intruders, blundering in upon some incomprehensible symphony of tireless musicians, who, with twittering elbows, performed night after night, on beetle-gut fiddles, before silent rows of invisible critics, of astute, infinitesimal Paul Rosenfelds, comfortably ensconced somewhere or other, quite close to us, under the vaulted mountain sky.

Then came the first fall of snow, and for months the juniper-trees, the fir-trees, the pine-trees, were mantled in white, so that when I stepped behind the barn, before bedtime, the little Colonial house would look like the glowing eye of a Kinokop lion on a desert of salt, or like a fiery ruby on a white shroud. Often the thermometer would drop below zero, and my beard would grow crisp with frost.

But what a rich, mellow quality the long evenings had, as we sat over a log-fire, reading from the edition of Burton's *Anatomy of Melancholy* that I had borrowed from Mr. Seldes! How the wind, like a famished timber-wolf with frosted belly, would howl round the corners of the house, denuding every apple-tree bough of its fell of snow, fells which that afternoon had given the branches the appearance of the antlers of innumerable stags come down to take shelter behind the wall! The cat would sit on the four-poster bed, watching its shadow on the wall; and across the boards of the attic above, where we had found, behind a heap of rubbish, the broken frame of an old spinning-wheel, tiny feet would scamper. That winter I came to understand the peculiar character, rude and simple, that belongs to the countryside of old America. Indeed, as I trudged through deep snow to the little village post-office, I knew that I was abroad in an environment such as had bred John Greenleaf Whittier. This impression would be strengthened on the occasions when Mr. De Graff would call me into his kitchen and sit talking with me over his stove in an atmosphere thick with the greasy smell produced by daily cooking of portions of the barren cow he had slaughtered at the time when the last few apples were being carried down from his orchard on the hill. The old man would tell me about the bear he had seen as he was coming back from Snake Quarry one evening, about a skunk he had trapped, or about the great blizzard in the Eighties, when the snow had drifted as high as the roof of his house. He also affirmed, when our conversation turned to sickness, that nothing was more beneficial for the kidneys than a jorum of juniper berries. I spoke of the spinning-wheel I had found in the attic, and at once he vigorously asserted that no wool was better than homespun wool, and showed me the socks he was wearing, which had been made out of the fleece of a ewe that he had bred on the farm, and that he remembered quite well, though it had been dead God knows how many years. One evening this good man, standing up in his homespuns, took out of his cupboard a Bible that had belonged to his great-grandfather, and on the title-page of which it was possible still to read, in a large, round hand, the words, 'De Graff, his Bible'. 'I would not part with that book,' he said, 'for five hundred, no, not for a thousand, dollars.'

In the white moonlight, as we lay in bed, we would sometimes be waked by the yapping of a fox, making its way across the sloping field, its stealthy paws scarcely leaving an indent on the crisp, sparkling floor over which they trod. Once I witnessed a very curious scene. I awoke suddenly to find myself watching a skunk dancing an arabesque on a level space in front of the well, a lonely, silent arabesque, for the benefit of our cat, which sat before it with pricked ears. And as I watched this animal in its gambols, rolling over and over, and frolicking sideways, I could not but feel astonishment that God should have conceived the whimsy of giving so quaint an animal so merry a heart.

Early in the new year came the total eclipse of the sun; and although this celestial phenomenon meant very little to Scofield Thayer, who observed it through a pair of Newmarket field-glasses, standing between Paul Rosenfeld and Dr. Watson, somewhere in Central Park, yet to us, in our lonely habitation, it was as if we had been permitted to glimpse the appalling accuracy of the material Universe with the startled eyes of sleepers suddenly awakened.

We stood on a heaped-up bank of snow, like two trapped rodents who, for once, in an illuminating moment, were allowed to see how the intricate hinges of their iron cage move. With wide-open eyes we stood there, while in all their august majesty the silent workings of the sidereal heavens lay exposed to our vision. If the voice of God himself, with husky, hallowed intonation, had come echoing over those frozen fields, we could not have been more amazed. This was something that reduced all our plaints about Death to an absurdity; this was something that reduced our lives to tiny markings on a level plain, markings of as little import as the markings left by the tails of the field-mice which I used to notice in the snow in front of the barn. There we stood, two live, intellectual souls, marooned in a mathematical cosmos from which there was no way of escape. And as the light of the sun went out, with my own eyes I saw the face of my mother, the tender earth, tremble as though she had been smitten. Small wonder that Mr. De Graff said to me, as with grave deliberation he collected

my letters, 'It makes a man think, to see such sights as that.'
As he uttered these words he gave me from under his steel
spectacles a puzzled, significant look, as though deep in his
heart he suspected the unwisdom of the modern world in
neglecting any longer to treat with reverence the musty
volume in his cupboard.

Little by little, signs of the spring appeared. First a dozen
honey-bees emerged from their hives and in a kind of hypnotised state hovered, like tiny hawks, about the warming
timber of the post-office door. A few weeks passed, and,
behold, once more the miracle had happened. Out of the
warped earth, out of the dead, soaked mould, sprang a
hundred dainty blossoms, blossoms more graceful, more
rare, than gleaming sea-shells. Anemones, foam-fair and
fairy-free, hepaticas, whose tender stems were covered
with tiny hairs, and spring-beauties that make all lovers
long 'to be in bed again'. And now, as the sun rose higher
and higher out of the wide Titian landscape, the summer
birds came back. The hoarse croaking of solitary crows
gave place to other sounds, and once again robins stepped
through the young spring grass, scattering dew-drops.
Indeed, there was no scrap of the ancient soil that was not
astir. One had only to lift up an old board, near where the
skunk danced, to find concealed, amid a hundred pale spears
struggling upwards, five naked lizards, still covered with
primeval slime.

At a particular period in this happy transition, when, in
spite of the sun-warmed days, it still froze at night, the
De Graffs hung buckets about the trunks of their sweet-

maples, so that as one walked by their farm there was scarcely a tree which had not a receptacle being filled, drop by drop, with pellucid sap.

But strange to say, the ancient enchantment of the season filled me only with restlessness. I had been in America for five years, for as long a time as I had spent in Africa; and now, as the swallow turns towards its familiar barn, as the cuckoo turns again to its buttercup pasture, so my heart turned toward England. Before this I had not the slightest wish to see my own land; but suddenly, in spite of—perhaps because of—all this beauty, my bowels languished for home, I longed for the smell of West Country hedges, for the smell of bramble-leaves and dock-leaves, and ditch-cool grasses, limp with the soft, enervating, odorous dampness of an Island night in June.

CHAPTER TWENTY-ONE

Departure

DURING MY last week in New York City, I went to spend an evening with Arthur Davison Ficke. The debonair, cosmopolitan rogue lived in low-raftered rooms at the bottom of a blind street, and it tickled my heart to see him there with his books all about him and a good decanter on the table. In the dim-lighted library, with his tall, slender lady at his side, one could not but commend a certain kind of worldly sagacity, capable of dealing sharply with life, so that even poor poets may on occasions loll at ease, as though in a fenced city. For I would have all my friends as sly and generous as my lord! Then would many of us poor wretches have harbourage in winter and no longer be fed on melon-rind and the meagre pips of pomegranates. Once, when I was spending an evening in the home of that other honourable defender of the oppressed, Dudley Field Malone, Ficke, for a whim, because forsooth it was a dark night, presented me, out of hand, with his own walking-stick, a gift that I treasure to this hour, and hope to treasure even unto the last days of my life, when under the providence of God, with my hair white as hoar frost, I totter out to the harvest field to watch another generation than mine gather in the golden grains of life.

Later in the evening, Edna St. Vincent Millay came in. I had not seen her for four years, but I found her unaltered.

She possessed the same fragile appearance, the same brittle, shell-like, petal-like appearance that had always set me marvelling. And her lovely leprechaun eyes, yellow-green in colour, had the same strange light in them that I had observed at first, like the light of baffled mistrust in the eyes of an infinitely desirable mermaiden who finds a crowd of alien creatures looking down at her through a glass-bottomed boat in some deep, seaweed-waving, rock-en-grottoed pool near the coral cliffs of Bermuda.

We spoke of the eclipse, and she referred to the forlorn aspect that the world wore during those moments of semi-darkness, making use of the word 'desolate' in such a way that even as I sat in my luxurious chair, I had a vision of the derelict earth, lost in space, but still carrying on its face its unhappy burden of men and cattle.

At last the hour came for our embarkation, and we sailed down the proud harbour, past the Battery, past the Statue of Liberty, past Staten Island. Little by little the embattled ambit of the great city faded behind us. I felt heavy at heart. With the English deck-steward fussing about with his chairs behind me, with his wooden, uncomfortable chairs, which even eight legs did not make long enough, I looked back at Manhattan, with a feeling of infinite regret and infinite devotion for this great new country that out of its careless largess had given me what my heart desired.

I cannot say that my travelling-companions contributed anything to my enthusiasm. They sat all day long in crowded rows, under the officious eyes of their avaricious servants, grumbling that the White Star Line should have thought fit to allow a negro company of actors and actresses berths outside the steerage. When half a dozen lusty blacks began to pipe to half a dozen negro girls in a hidden part of the deck, their indignation knew no bounds. I, for one, did not share their prejudices, but liked very well to see these little wenches, limber and light, dance under the moon. Indeed, their singsong refrain, 'Grab yo' girls, don't get rough', kept repeating itself in my mind long after I had fled to a deserted deck in the steerage, where I found I could escape from the obsequious eyes of the stewards, and from the mean eyes of the other passengers, who made me feel, as I walked past them, with my old plaid shawl that used to belong to Edward Fitz Gerald, over my shoulders, as though I were being gazed at by a flock of carnivorous sheep.

CHAPTER TWENTY-TWO

A Headland Refuge

WE CAME up the Channel at midnight; so that it was not until the hour before dawn that I was waked by the lowering of the anchor, and looked out of my porthole at England. There she lay in her unrivalled loveliness, virginal and unspoilt. The sea that encircled her rocks, that lapped against the smooth pebbles of her beaches, was still and calm, as still and calm to look upon as the flocks which I could see grazing in the small green fields of Devonshire. At that unequalled hour, with a fishing-boat gently rocking against a sky already streaked with red, with the cold seaside air coming in through the round brass-bound aperture, I was able to contemplate my native land with detachment. There she lay, in her sturdy beauty, with her cottages dotting the hillside like moss-grown, lichened stones, with her sloping uplands golden with gorse, and with her elm trees already out in tender May-time leaf.

By the following evening I was on the White Nore, the wildest, proudest headland of all the Dorset coast. Except for the hum of a bumblebee, sipping honey from a patch of vipers-bugloss, there was no sound save that of the sea murmuring round rocks six hundred feet below.

To the left were downs, rising and falling, one behind the other, as far as St. Aldhelm's Head. Everywhere against the skyline were visible the immemorial burial mounds of the men of the old time. I saw also in the distance the hill which I knew overlooked Corfe Castle—Corfe Castle, with its Norman keep haunted by shining jackdaws, still standing after eight hundred years, its very robeguards, the turreted drought of the medieval lords and ladies, still visible above the moat. Yet all that had happened to me since I last looked for tracks outside the badger-hole in Middle Bottom, all that I had seen, and all that I had heard, had been contained, so I found, within the compass of the lifetime of a cat, of my brother's sandy cat, Peter Paul, old now, it is true, but still able to enjoy an afternoon's sleep in the long grass under the sycamore.

I walked to the very edge of the cliff and looked over. Far below, at the foot of a ledge grown with samphire, I could see a dozen foolish guillemots drying their wings in the last rays of the sinking sun. On a ledge much higher up, not more, so I judged, than a hundred feet from where I was standing, a cormorant sat becking at me with its long black-green head outstretched, for all the world like Chaucer's pardoner. And because of a certain quality in that evening air, a quality nameless, absolute, indefinable, I knew that for a surety I was home once more.

THE END